Representative American Speeches 2006–2007

Edited by Jennifer Curry, Paul McCaffrey, and Lynn M. Messina

The Reference Shelf
Volume 79 • Number 6

The H. W. Wilson Company
2007

The Reference Shelf

The books in this series contain reprints of articles, excerpts from books, addresses on current issues, and studies of social trends in the United States and other countries. There are six separately bound numbers in each volume, all of which are usually published in the same calendar year. Numbers one through five are each devoted to a single subject, providing background information and discussion from various points of view and concluding with a subject index and comprehensive bibliography that lists books, pamphlets, and abstracts of additional articles on the subject. The final number of each volume is a collection of recent speeches, and it contains a cumulative speaker index. Books in the series may be purchased individually or on subscription.

Library of Congress has cataloged this serial title as follows:
Representative American speeches. 1937 / 38–
    New York, H. W. Wilson Co.™
        v. 21 cm.—The Reference Shelf
Annual
Indexes:
    Author index: 1937/38–1959/60, with 1959/60;
    1960/61–1969/70, with 1969/70; 1970/71–1979/80,
    with 1979/80; 1980/81–1989/90, 1990.
Editors: 1937/38–1958/59, A. C. Baird.—1959/60–1969/70, L. Thonssen.—1970/71–1979/80, W. W. Braden.—1980/81–1994/95, O. Peterson.—1995/96–1998/99, C. M. Logue and J. DeHart.—1999/2000–2002/2003, C. M. Logue and L. M. Messina.—2003/2004–2005/2006, C. M. Logue, L. M. Messina, and J. DeHart. —2006/2007– , J. Currie, P. McCaffrey, L. M. Messina.
    ISSN 0197-6923 Representative American speeches.
        1. Speeches, addresses, etc., American. 2. Speeches, addresses, etc.
        I. Baird, Albert Craig, 1883–1979 ed. II. Thonssen, Lester, 1904–
        III. Braden, Waldo Warder, 1911–1991 ed.
        IV. Peterson, Owen, 1924– ed. V. Logue, Calvin McLeod, 1935– ,
        Messina, Lynn M., and DeHart, Jean, eds. VI. Series.
PS668.B3   815.5082   38-27962
                                                        MARC-S
    Library of Congress [8503r85] rev4

Cover: NEW YORK - MAY 25: Former U.S. Vice President and Academy Award winner Al Gore appears at Barnes and Noble to support his new book "The Assault On Reason" on May 25, 2007 in New York City. (Photo by Brad Barket/Getty Images)

Visit H. W. Wilson's Web site: www.hwwilson.com

Printed in the United States of America

The Reference Shelf®

Contents

Preface

As President George W. Bush's second term draws to an end and presidential candidates begin ramping up their campaigns, Americans across the political spectrum are considering the future of their country. This volume of *Representative American Speeches* examines many of the issues that will be debated in the upcoming presidential election: education (particularly as it relates to the economy), the United States' place in the increasingly globalized marketplace, health care reform, the role of immigration in our society, and global climate change.

The first two chapters in this collection are closely intertwined. There is an undeniable relationship—particularly in today's highly technological workplace—between the quality of education and both the economic viability of a nation and the security of its workers. According to recent census data, American adults with advanced degrees earn four times more than those with less than a high school diploma. Consequently, as more and more American manufacturing and unskilled jobs move overseas, the wage gap is likely to increase further. Though most citizens and politicians agree that to counteract this trend the country's underperforming schools must be improved, how best to improve them remains in dispute.

Much as with education reform, no consensus has emerged as to how to fix the nation's ailing health care system, the focal point of the speeches in the third chapter. In the United States, comprehensive health care is mostly beyond the reach of those who do not receive health insurance from their employer or through government programs—and the number of uninsured Americans continues to climb, growing from 44.8 million in 2005 to 47 million in 2006. Even those who are covered often find their insurance in some way lacking, especially when faced with higher deductibles, exorbitant copayments, and bureaucratic red tape. Indeed, having health insurance does not shield one from the financial peril of a medical crisis. A study conducted by Harvard University found that of the nearly 1.5 million personal bankruptcies declared in the United States in 2001, over half were so called "medical bankruptcies," resulting from doctors' bills, lost wages due to illness, and other health-care–related expenses. Of those who declared bankruptcy, most were insured and middle class at the outset of their medical emergency. Consequently, while the United States has the technology and human capital to provide the highest level of health care in the world, we nevertheless spend significantly more and yet are in poorer health than our counterparts in western Europe, where socialized medicine—government-provided or subsidized health care—is the norm. Given the uneasiness many Americans have with the European model, the prospects of such a system developing in the United

States remain distant, though if the situation continues to deteriorate and no market-based solution emerges, such a model might become increasingly appealing.

Polls conducted by the Pew Research Center have found that while the majority of Americans have a favorable attitude toward free markets and globalizing trade, they also believe that immigration should be further restricted and controlled. This latter sentiment can be partially attributed to the fallout from the terrorist attacks of September 11, 2001, as the rather porous border between the United States and Mexico presents a security risk. On the other hand, Americans have long debated whether the hundreds of thousands of undocumented immigrants who enter the country every year—as either seasonal workers or permanent residents—pose a net benefit or liability to the economy.

Speeches in the final chapter examine the debate over global warming. Upon announcing that it would award the 2007 Nobel Peace Prize to former Vice President Al Gore and the Intergovernmental Panel on Climate Change (IPCC) for "their efforts to build up and disseminate greater knowledge about man-made climate change," the Nobel committee declared, "Thousands of scientists and officials from over one hundred countries have collaborated to achieve greater certainty as to the scale of the warming. Whereas in the 1980s global warming seemed to be merely an interesting hypothesis, the 1990s produced firmer evidence in its support." Nevertheless, global climate change remains a politically contentious issue in certain circles—particularly in the United States, as is demonstrated by the speeches featured in this chapter.

In conclusion, we would like to extend our sincerest gratitude to the men and women who allowed us to reprint their speeches in this book. In addition we would like to offer particular thanks to Richard Stein for his invaluable assistance in compiling this collection.

December 2007

I. EDUCATION

Science Education in the United States Reaches a Crossroad

Martin C. Jischke

President, Purdue University, West Lafayette, IN, 2000–06; born Chicago, IL, August 7, 1941; B.S., Illinois Institute of Technology, physics with honors, 1963; M.S., Massachusetts Institute of Technology (MIT), 1964; engineer, Rand Corporation, Santa Monica, CA, 1965; Ph.D., MIT, 1968; from assistant professor to professor, School of Aerospace and Mechanical Engineering, University of Oklahoma, 1968–75; research engineer, Battelle, 1970; research fellow, Donald W. Douglas Laboratories, Richland, WA, 1971; research fellow, National Aeronautics and Space Administration, 1973; White House fellow, special assistant to the secretary of transportation, 1975–76; director, School of Aerospace and Mechanical Engineering, University of Oklahoma, 1977–81; dean, College of Engineering, University of Oklahoma, 1981–86; interim president, University of Oklahoma, 1985; chancellor, University of Missouri, Rolla, 1986–91; president, Iowa State University, 1991–2000.

Editor's introduction: Before embarking on a successful career as a college administrator, Martin C. Jischke was a specialist in fluid dynamics and held a research fellowship at NASA. As such, he understands firsthand the importance of education in science and technology. While serving as Purdue's president he oversaw an ambitious fund-raising campaign to pay for an interdisciplinary complex called Discovery Park, which serves as a home to research in bioscience, manufacturing, nanotechnology, and Internet-based entrepreneurship. In the following speech, delivered to the Lafayette, IN, Rotary, Jischke expresses his concern that the United States is "falling behind in the production of people in science, engineering, technology and math."

Martin C. Jischke's speech: Good afternoon. Thank you for the opportunity to speak with you today.

I am a Rotarian. I believe in the work that Rotary is doing.

Rotary efforts have important focuses on youth, education and international exchanges. That is why I have chosen this opportunity to talk with you today about the future of our nation and the dreams for our future.

We are at a crossroads in our nation as we enter a century that we know will be dominated by science, engineering, technology and education. A convergence of science, technology and engineering is taking place. And this convergence is about to change the world.

Delivered on January 24, 2006, at Lafayette, IN. Reprinted with permission.

At Purdue today, we are working in the nanoscale in a brand-new $58 million nanotechnology center.

Nanotechnology is a science in which new materials and tiny structures are built atom-by-atom, or molecule-by-molecule. We are talking about computers smaller than your wristwatch.

We have linked our nanotechnology center with a new $15 million bioscience center.

In the biosciences we are talking about placing devices into your body that not only will determine what is wrong with you—they will fix it!

It is exciting and incredible!

And yet, at a point in time when science, technology and engineering are opening all these incredible potentials the United States is falling behind in the production of graduates in these fields.

Indeed, if current trends continue, by 2010, only four years from now, more than 90 percent of all scientists and engineers in the world will live in Asia.

This is a technology deficit. It is being called a "gathering storm."

Just as people on our Gulf Coast must prepare for a gathering hurricane before it makes landfall we must address this technology deficit before it is too late. And the force for strengthening our nation in this gathering storm lies in education.

We think of the United States today as the land of promise and opportunity. And it is.

Education is the cornerstone of that promise and opportunity. But it has not always been within the grasp of common men and women.

In the 18th century, when this nation was founded, educational opportunities were limited.

The real promise and opportunity that are the hallmarks of this nation emerged from a consensus that grew among the people to make higher education available to everyone.

In the mid-1800s, Justin Morrill, a Vermont congressman, led a movement that believed higher education should not be limited to an elite group defined by wealth. Morrill, and others like him, believed higher education should be available to all the masses of people.

It was a turning point in history when President Abraham Lincoln signed the Morrill Land-Grant Act of 1862. That act provided the means for states to create new universities dedicated to learning, discovery, and engagement—all for the public good.

Within eight years, 37 states had initiated these institutions of higher learning—among them, Purdue.

Today, there are more than 100 land-grant colleges and universities swept across the breadth of this great country offering promise and opportunity to all.

But still, by 1940 only two out of five Americans had been educated past the eighth grade. In 1940, only 16 percent of Americans 18 to 21 years of age were enrolled in universities.

Today, almost 67 percent of U.S. high school graduates from the class of 2004 enrolled in colleges and universities.

This dramatic change in higher education was sparked by the G.I. Bill at the end of World War II. The G.I. Bill provided funds making it possible to educate huge numbers of individuals who never before even considered attending college.

The G.I. Bill educated a generation.

The enormous economic growth and social advancements that fueled the 20th Century took place predominantly after World War II. That is when the G.I. Bill educated people in the emerging technologies of the day.

Who were these people?

They were people like Kenneth Johnson, who grew up on remote farms in Arkansas and Missouri and went to a one-room school-house surrounded by mud. He came to Purdue on the G.I. Bill, graduated with a degree in engineering, and went on to help revolutionize airplane engine technology working for General Electric.

They were people like Billy Christensen, who finished his studies at Purdue in 1950 on the G.I. Bill and took a job with a punch card company. He went on to become vice president and general manager of the international arm of that company—IBM.

> The G.I. Bill was an investment in people and education that has paid for itself many times over.

They were people like Bill Rose, who barely survived the Depression before he went to war and then came to Purdue on the G.I. Bill fresh out of the Navy. He graduated and took a job in the Joint Long-Range Proving Ground, at the Banana River Naval Station. We know it today as the Kennedy Space Center.

The G.I. Bill was an investment in people and education that has paid for itself many times over.

The Morrill Land-Grant Act of the 19th century and the G.I. Bill of the 20th were education-focused legislation that changed America. And there was one more.

In 1957 the Russians beat us into space with Sputnik. Many of you remember this and the widespread fears of the time that American was falling behind in science, engineering and technology.

In response to this the United States launched a satellite in 1958 and also determined to put a man into space.

The space race was on.

But we did more than that. We invested in education. We invested to ensure that a generation of young people—people like you and me—would be sparked by the potentials and possibilities that emerge from science, technology and engineering

In 1958 Congress passed the National Defense Education Act.

The National Defense Education Act included: support for loans to college students, the improvement of science, mathematics, and foreign language instruction in elementary and secondary schools, graduate fellowships, and vocational-technical training.

What was the impact of all of this?

Several years ago, the National Academy of Engineering listed the top engineering achievements of the 20th century. They are a stunning glimpse into the progress of human civilization. Purdue engineer Neil Armstrong was the keynote speaker when the list was announced.

Here are the top achievements that changed the way we lived and worked in the 20th century: electrification, automobiles, airplanes, water supply, electronics, radio and television, agricultural mechanization, computers, telephones, air conditioning, interstate highways, the Internet, imaging, health technologies, petrochemical technologies, lasers and fiber optics, nuclear technologies, and high-performance materials.

Close your eyes and try to imagine our world today without these contributions from engineers as well as those from scientists. These are advancements that took us from the horse-and-buggy age at the dawn of the 20th century to the space age and the exploration of Mars and other planets at the dawn of the 21st.

It is clear that American investments in higher education—and most especially investments in science, math, engineering and technology—played a major role in creating this great nation and all the comforts and benefits that we enjoy.

But we have lapsed, and lapsed dramatically in a remarkably short period of time.

Twenty years ago, the United States, Japan and China each graduated a similar number of engineers and more than twice the total coming out of South Korea.

By the year 2000: Chinese engineering graduates had increased 161 percent to 207,500; Japanese engineering graduates had increased 42 percent to 103,200; South Korean engineering graduates had increased 140 percent to 56,500; and credible and in fact very conservative estimates place India's production of engineers today at more than 100,000 per year.

Meanwhile U.S. engineering graduates have declined 20 percent—to 59,500.

A recent study out of Duke University has challenged some of these statistics by comparing quality of education and the number of years of training to receive an engineering degree in various nations.

But it has not challenged the heart of this message: We are falling behind in the production of people in science, engineering, technology and math, which is at the core of all three.

Our middle school and high school students are unprepared in math and science and correspondingly uninterested in these careers.

Of the nearly 1.1 million U.S. high school seniors who took the college entrance exam in 2002, less than 6 percent had plans to study engineering. That is a 33 percent decrease from 10 years earlier.

Meanwhile, more than 50 percent of the current U.S. science and engineering workforce is approaching retirement.

What is the impact of this?

New York Times columnist and author Thomas Friedman writes that a new world has emerged a "flat world," leveled by technology.

Norman R. Augustine, retired Chairman and Chief Executive Officer of Lockheed Martin Corporation chaired the Committee on Prospering in the Global Economy of the 21st Century. This was a committee of the National Academies, the advisors to the nation on science, engineering and medicine.

Here are some of the points made by Norman Augustine in his testimony October 20 to the U.S. House of Representatives Committee on Science:

"U.S. companies each morning receive software that was written in India overnight in time to be tested in the U.S. and returned to India for further production that same evening—making the 24-hour workday a practicality.

"Drawings for American architectural firms are produced in Brazil. U.S. firms' call centers are based in India—where employees are now being taught to speak with a Midwestern accent. U.S. hospitals have X-rays and CAT scans read by radiologists in Australia and India. Accounting firms in the U.S. have clients' tax returns prepared by experts in India. Visitors to an office not far from the White House are greeted by a receptionist on a flat screen display who controls access to the building and arranges contacts. She is in Pakistan.

"For the cost of one engineer in the United States, a company can hire 11 in India.

"Chemical companies closed 70 facilities in the U.S. in 2004, and have tagged 40 more for shutdown. Of 120 new chemical plants being built around the world with price tags of $1 billion or more, one is in the U.S. and 50 are in China.

"The United States today is a net importer of high-technology products."

Just as there is a convergence of technologies, there is a convergence of four trends impacting our nation today.

First, we are experiencing a decline in the number of American students enrolling in our engineering and science programs.

Second, we are experiencing a decline in federal research support for engineering and the physical sciences. Since 1970, U.S. funding for basic research in the physical sciences has declined by half as a percentage of the gross domestic product.

Third, since 9/11 we have experienced a decline in international enrollment. We are losing many top students from the around the world who not only have invigorated our academic programs but have challenged and motivated our American students.

And fourth, other nations—especially in Asia—are aggressively increasing research funding, enrollments and the quality of programs at universities.

China, for example, plans to increase the proportion of science spending devoted to basic research by more than 200 percent in the next 10 years.

At Purdue we had the first computer science department in the nation. Undergraduate enrollment in that program has dropped 47 percent in four years.

Purdue is a top 10 engineering college. Every year applications to our engineering graduate programs decline another 25 to 30 percent.

The shortfall of U.S. students and workers in science and engineering has traditionally been met by internationals who studied in the U.S. and often joined our workforce.

Where would we be without them?

Thirty percent of Purdue faculty members are foreign-born—including 47.9 percent of our engineering and science faculty.

In a post–9/11 world, the way people in other nations perceive us, coupled with our immigration policies, is negatively impacting international enrollment and the U.S. international workforce. International enrollment, after many years of steady growth, dropped 2.4 percent two years ago and 1.3 percent last year.

The decline in international enrollment now seems to be slowing. We are hopeful we have turned the corner.

Purdue ranks third in the nation in international enrollment behind only the University of Southern California and the University of Illinois. But even as we work very hard to increase our international enrollment, we continue to face enormous competition for international students from Great Britain, New Zealand, Australia and Canada.

I have also been to India and China in the past year to see the tremendous advances in their universities and research. The speed of change abroad, especially China and India, is quite amazing. At Tsinghua, the MIT of China, a whole new south campus is being built with both government and private resources.

Similar changes are taking place at Fudan and elsewhere.

And these universities are hiring Chinese and others from the United States. The first Western department head at Tsinghua is a Purdue faculty member.

Purdue and other universities have implemented programs reaching out to high school, junior high and grade school students to interest them in science and engineering. We have launched programs to increase the number of teachers in these fields and to improve our curricula. We are looking at the engineering needs of the 21st century and will redesign our program to train that person.

The National Academies report, "Rising Above the Gathering Storm: Energizing and Employing America for a Brighter Economic Future," proposes a number of initiatives to meet the technology deficit.

The recommendations include awarding scholarships to recruiting science and mathematics teachers. In return for the scholarships, the students would commit to five years of teaching in public K–12 schools.

Other proposals call for programs to upgrade the skills of current math and science teachers. The recommendations include strengthening our commitment to long-term basic research. The recommendations also suggest investments in "high-risk, high pay-off" research.

In spite of all these concerns, American higher education continues to be the best in the world. We can meet and overcome these challenges. It is not too late.

We can maintain our worldwide lead even as other countries invest heavily to build up their own high-technology sectors.

We absolutely can do it. But to succeed, we will need a national consensus, just as we needed popular support for the Land Grant Act, the G.I. Bill and the National Defense Education Act. We can inspire a whole new generation of young people to the incredible opportunities in science, engineering, technology and math.

And the returns on our investment will be gigantic.

It will be a stronger nation and a world filled with breath-taking advances in medicine, science and engineering—breakthroughs that are beyond our dreams today.

President Dwight Eisenhower was not an engineer. But he certainly understood the importance of engineering in everything from the D-Day invasion to building the interstate highway system, which he launched in the 1950s.

President Eisenhower said: "Engineers build for the future, not merely for the needs of men (and women), but for their dreams as well."

The dreams for the future of America are studying in our schools today.

It is our job to inspire and to provide them with the resources they need to succeed. We must begin building for tomorrow today! With your help we will succeed.

Thank you.

The Importance of Education

Roger W. Ferguson, Jr.

Chairman, Swiss Re America Holding Corporation, 2006– ; born Washington, D.C., October 28, 1951; B.A., economics, Harvard University, 1973; J.D., Harvard University, 1979; Ph.D., economics, Harvard University, 1981; attorney, Davis, Polk, and Wardell, New York City, 1981–84; director of research and information, McKinsey and Company, 1984–97; member, Board of Governors, Federal Reserve System, 1997–99; vice chairman, Board of Governors, Federal Reserve System, 1999–2006.

Editor's introduction: In a study conducted by the U.S. Department of Education, which Roger W. Ferguson, Jr., cites in the address below, researchers found that "blacks' relative educational achievement during elementary and secondary school appeared to be highly correlated with their relative success in the academy and the economy." Recognizing the relationship between education and economic performance among all ethnic groups in the United States, Ferguson argues, in this speech commemorating Black History Month, which he delivered at Johns Hopkins University's Applied Physics Laboratory, that addressing disparities in education is pivotal to securing "the economic well-being of African Americans."

Roger W. Ferguson, Jr.'s speech: I am pleased to have the opportunity to be part of the Applied Physics Laboratory's commemoration of Black History Month. Your theme, "Celebrating Community: A Tribute to Black Technical, Educational, and Social/Civic Institutions," aptly highlights a number of the key building blocks that have enabled many African Americans to fulfill their personal dreams. In that regard, I would like to focus my talk today on education—its importance and its ongoing role in economic achievement.

As members of an organization dedicated to cutting-edge scientific research and development, you undoubtedly deeply appreciate the ongoing need for our nation's workforce to embody advanced levels of training. Investment in human capital—as we economists like to call it—is critical to generating products and services with high economic value. Today, much of that high-value output demands workers with the creativity, cognitive abilities, and skills to interact with challenging technologies. In addition, ongoing innovation requires workers to be flexible and to be willing to view education as a life-long commitment. In short, an educated workforce is a must if our economy is to continue to enjoy significant gains in productivity and living standards.

Delivered on February 24, 2006, at Laurel, Maryland.

At the same time, the link between education and individual economic success is well documented. An investment in education is associated with a higher probability of employment. For African Americans, a college degree can substantially narrow the longstanding gap between their labor market experiences and those of whites. Last year, for example, when the national unemployment rate averaged 5.1 percent, the jobless rate for black adults (25 years and older) with a bachelor's degree or higher was 3.5 percent; for white adults, the jobless rate was 2 percent. For persons with only a high school diploma, both the rates of joblessness and the disparity between the rate for blacks and that for whites were greater: an unemployment rate of 8.5 percent for blacks versus 4 percent for whites.

Perhaps more indicative of the economic value of education, workers with college degrees earn an education premium, and that premium has risen over the past twenty-five years. Most economists have found that an additional year of schooling typically raises an individual's earning power between 8 and 15 percent. Recent studies show that four years of college boost earnings about 65 percent.[1]

> We have made some progress in opening doors to education for African Americans; we must make more.

Clearly, economic achievement and educational achievement are intertwined. For that reason, education is at the heart of efforts to promote equal opportunity for all Americans. We have made some progress in opening doors to education for African Americans; we must make more.

As I reflect on the educational attainment of black Americans, I would say that the news is still mixed. The percentage of African Americans aged 25 to 29 who have completed high school or obtained a GED remains on an uptrend. But the improvements slowed over the 1990s, and in 2004 it remained, at close to 89 percent, short of the rate for non-Hispanic white youth, which was just over 93 percent.[2]

One important factor in the uptrend in high-school completion has been a corresponding downtrend in the high-school dropout rate for African Americans. Here again, however, the improvement has been slower recently than in the 1970s and 1980s. In 2003, 6.3 percent of black students in grades 10 to 12 left school during the year—down from the over-the-year dropout rate of 9.7 percent in 1981 but little changed from the rate in 1991.[3] For white high schoolers, the dropout rate between 2000 and 2001 was 4.1 percent.

Economists have identified a number of reasons for the racial gap in dropout rates, including lower expected returns to education because of discrimination in the job market and the lower quality of schools attended by blacks. Clearly, raising the quality of our elementary and secondary schools is a longstanding goal, and the potential economic and social payoffs seem likely to be high. Research has shown that improving school conditions in the South

from the early to the middle part of the twentieth century contributed significantly to greater school completion rates by African
Americans.[4] Other findings suggest that the support and encouragement that students receive from their families and communities can
also help keep students engaged in school. In recent years, a number of economists, including staff members of the Federal Reserve
Bank of Minneapolis, have argued that intensive pre-school programs can help to build important noncognitive skills, such as per-
sistence and motivation and, as a result, have large private and
public net benefits.[5]

Of course our job is not done when our students reach high school
graduation—indeed, in today's economy, it is only just beginning.
Our goal must be to see that our investments in motivating and educating students in our homes and in the elementary and secondary
schools provide the students with the ability to pursue the advanced
education and training that today's labor market values so highly.

Certainly, the trends in college-attendance by blacks have been
positive in recent years, but compared with the uptrend in
high-school completion, progress in college completion among African Americans has unfortunately been relatively slow. The percentage of the black population aged 25 to 35 that has completed four
years of college more than doubled between 1970 and 2000, from 6.5
percent to 15 percent. However, completion rates for young white
adults, which were already much higher, climbed even more rapidly—to almost 33 percent in 2000.[6]

The difference in college completion by race reflects both lower
rates of college enrollment and lower rates of graduation by African
Americans. Of African Americans aged 18 to 24, the percentage
enrolled in college is 10 percentage points lower than the percentage
of non-Hispanic whites enrolled.[7] The difference in graduation rates
for those students who enroll in college is particularly striking. Of
those students who enrolled as first-time students at a four-year
institution in the 1995–96 academic year, approximately 62 percent
of whites had completed a bachelor's degree by 2001, whereas only
43 percent of blacks had done so.[8]

Researchers offer several potential explanations for the difference
in college graduation rates by race. The extent to which family
income or borrowing costs significantly constrain the decision to
enroll in college has been hotly debated by economists.[9] The common ground in the debate seems to be that needy students who are
capable should be helped financially. But money alone is not the
answer; students must receive the support, encouragement, and
preparation from their teachers, families, and communities that will
make the transition from high school to college successful. Research
has shown that blacks have a higher rate of college attendance than
whites and a similar rate of college completion when the comparison
is made across individuals with similar educational achievement in

high school.[10] This finding provides yet another reason for greater investment in the quality of secondary schools. Such investment may increase not only rates of high-school graduation but also rates of college completion.

As I noted earlier, the linkage between education and economic opportunity is typically measured by the relationship between education and earnings. Earnings are an important measure of one's success in the labor market, but broader measures of income and ultimately net worth are even more significant yardsticks for gauging the financial health of households. The Federal Reserve's Survey of Consumer Finances, which collects data every three years on the balance sheets of American families, provides comprehensive information on household income, assets, and liabilities.[11] Data from the most recent survey show that, from 2001 to 2004, real (that is, inflation-adjusted) family income was little changed for both African American and non-Hispanic white households. And the gap between median incomes for the two groups remained quite large. Specifically, the median income of black households was about $29,000—only 58 percent of the median for non-Hispanic white households. The gap was somewhat narrower among households headed by an individual with a college degree; median income for African American households in this group was close to $54,000—75 percent of the median for non-Hispanic whites. Although black households have gained ground over the past decade, income inequality continues to be a concern. Lower income makes it more difficult for black families to acquire assets and to create wealth.

The 2004 results show that economic progress for blacks, as measured by real net worth, has been substantial over the fifteen years that the surveys have been conducted. Real median net worth for African-American households in 2004, at $20,400, was more than three and one-half times as great as it was in 1989. That said, the wealth gap between blacks and non-Hispanic whites, whose median real net worth stood at $140,700 in 2004, remains sizable. A substantial part of the wealth gap between black and non-Hispanic white families is associated with their ownership of assets. Although the racial wealth gap is significant at the top of the wealth distribution, a more important difference is that a much greater proportion of African-American families than whites have zero or near-zero real net worth.

The increase in ownership of nonfinancial assets for black households in recent years occurred primarily in residences, other real estate, and privately held businesses. Because none of these types of assets is owned by a large share of black families, any wealth gains arising from them will not be widely distributed across black families. Nonetheless, blacks continued to make progress in homeownership in 2004. As is the case regardless of race, the home is typically a family's largest and most important asset. Homeownership is one of the cornerstones of wealth creation and is generally associated with a range of socially desirable outcomes, including better schools, less crime, and greater neighborhood stability. For these and other reasons, increasing the rate of homeownership has been a long-standing national priority. Of course, because we are interested not simply in homeownership or the value of homes but in net worth, an important consideration in terms of wealth creation is the amount of equity that families have in their homes—that is the difference between the value of the home and any debt secured by it. Over the most recent survey period, during which property values have risen rapidly, the median value of home equity for African-American homeowners increased an impressive 24 percent.

Business ownership, too, remains an important avenue of wealth creation for African Americans. The median net worth of black families with business assets was about $174,000 in 2004, a level more than eight times the median net worth for all black families. Furthermore, the survey results show far less inequality in median net worth and income between black and non-Hispanic white business owners than between black and non-Hispanic white families overall.

All told, the findings from our most recent survey, along with the other trends that I discussed earlier, highlight noticeable gains in the economic well-being of African Americans. However, they also clearly show that much more needs to be accomplished, and I believe that education is the key to further progress.

Given the importance of education in today's economy, I was encouraged to see that the Applied Physics Laboratory is committed to a number of programs that engage minority students at all levels of schooling. These programs are aimed at developing a commitment to lifelong learning—beginning with an introduction to math, science, and technology in our primary and secondary schools. In light of the differences in college completion rates I noted earlier, I was glad to see that APL offers internships for talented minority undergraduates in computer science and engineering that give them opportunities to do research and to be mentored by professionals in their fields and that it provides support for graduate study in engineering.

I was also interested to learn that many of your undergraduate interns are students from historically black colleges and universities (HBCUs). To borrow a phrase from Juan Williams, those very special institutions have for decades had as their central mission helping African Americans "find a way or make one."[12] And, even though black enrollment at other colleges and universities has risen over time, HBCUs continue to account for more than one-fifth of all bachelor's degrees awarded to African Americans.[13] Among those schools and their graduates are many with a longstanding commitment to scientific and technical education, dating from George Washington Carver's tenure at Tuskegee to Julian Earls's work at NASA. In this region, we are fortunate to have a fine group of HBCUs: Howard and Morgan State, both highly regarded across a range of curricula; Bowie State, which specializes in training black students for masters degrees in computer science; Maryland Eastern Shore, with its emphasis on marine and environmental science; and Coppin State, known for its nurturing of students as they build the fundamental skills that allow them to move on to more-advanced work.

Although most of my remarks today have centered on the economic value of education, I want to emphasize that a good education is much more than just the classroom-based learning of facts, or even the skill of critical thinking. Formal education is just the starting point for a lifetime of learning and doing. And a truly outstanding education is one that instills in students moral values and ethical behaviors. In striving to encourage our students to do "well," we must not forsake our responsibility to give them a solid grounding in those topics that will help them do "good." You may be surprised to hear that even the economics profession—well-known for its hard-headed assumption of rational actors pursuing their own self interest—has in the past few decades focused on the role of moral and cooperative behaviors in leading to better economic outcomes. The accounting and corporate governance scandals in recent years have revealed how costly such unethical and opportunistic business dealings can be, potentially to all of us.

Let me close by saying that the economy of the United States depends greatly on an educated workforce—one with the skills to tackle new ideas and new technologies, one in which morals and ethics are deeply instilled, and one with a love of learning, exploring, and questioning that lasts a lifetime. The African-American community's commitment to education as a path to equal opportunity dates back at least to Frederick Douglass. We all must resolve to keep that longstanding commitment strong.

Footnotes

1. Robert Topel, "The Private and Social Values of Education (891 KB PDF)," Federal Reserve Bank of Cleveland Conference on Education and Economic Development, November 19, 2004.

2. Mary Ann Fox, Brooke A. Connolly, and Thomas D. Snyder, *Trends in the Well-Being of American Youth* (592 KB PDF), U.S. Department of Education, National Center for Educational Statistics (November 2005).

3. Philip Kaufman, Martha Naomi Alt, and Christopher D. Chapman, *Dropout Rates in the United States: 2001* (369 KB PDF), U.S. Department of Education, National Center for Educational Statistics (November 2004).

4. David Card and Alan Krueger, "School Quality and Black-White Relative Wage Differentials," *Quarterly Journal of Economics*, 1992.

5. James J. Heckman and Pedro Carneiro, "Human Capital Policy," in James J. Heckman and Alan B. Krueger, eds., *Inequality in America: What Role for Human Capital Policies?* (The MIT Press, 2003), and Rob Grunewald and Arthur Rolnick, "A Proposal for Achieving High Returns on Early Childhood Development," Federal Reserve Bank of Minneapolis, May 2005.

6. Yolanda Kodrzycki, "College Completion Gaps between Blacks and Whites: What Accounts for the Regional Differences," *New England Economic Review*, Federal Reserve Bank of Boston, First Quarter 2004.

7. U.S. Census Bureau of the Census, Education and Social Stratification Branch, Current Population Survey Report, Historical Tables, Table A-5a (Excel file).

8. U.S. Department of Education, *Digest of Education Statistics*, Table 311, National Center for Educational Statistics, 2004.

9. Refer to, for example, Thomas Kane, "College Entry by Blacks Since 1970: The Role of College Costs, Family Background, and the Returns to Education," *Journal of Political Economy*, October 1994; J. Bradford DeLong, Claudia Goldin, and Lawrence F. Kartz, "Sustaining U.S. Economic Growth," in Henry J. Aaron, James M. Lindsay, and Pietro S. Nivola, eds., *Agenda for the Nation* (The Brookings Institution, 2003); Steven V. Cameron and James J. Heckman, "Can Tuition Policy Combat Rising Wage Inequality," in Marvin Kosters (ed.), *Financing College Education: Government Policies and Educational Priorities* (American Enterprise Institute, 1999).

10. U.S. Department of Education, "Educational Achievement and Black-White Inequality," National Center for Education Statistics, July 2001.

11. Brian K. Bucks., Arthur B. Kennickell, and Kevin B. Moore, "Recent Changes in U.S. Family Finances: Evidence from the 2001 and 2004 Survey of Consumer Finances (444 KB PDF)," *Federal Reserve Bulletin*, February 2006.

12. Juan Williams, *I'll Find a Way or Make One: A Tribute to Historically Black Colleges and Universities* (HarperCollins, 2004).

13. Stephen Provasnik, Linda L. Shafer, and Thomas D. Snyder, *Historically Black Colleges and Universities, 1976 to 2001*, U.S. Department of Education, National Center for Education Statistics, September 2004.

Remarks on the Fifth Anniversary of the *No Child Left Behind Act*

Margaret Spellings

U.S. secretary of education, 2005– ; born Ann Arbor, MI, November 30, 1957; B.A., University of Houston, 1979; aide to the Texas legislature; director of select committee on education for Texas Governor William P. Clements, Jr.; lobbyist and associate executive director, Texas Association of School Boards; political director, George W. Bush's campaign for governor of Texas, 1994; senior adviser on education policy to Governor Bush, 1995– 2000; domestic policy adviser to President George W. Bush, 2001–04.

Editor's introduction: Secretary Margaret Spellings was one of the principal authors of the No Child Left Behind Act, which she describes in the following address as a law "meant to shine the spotlight on" underperforming schools, increasing accountability. Delivered before a gathering of national business and education leaders at the U.S. Chamber of Commerce, the speech highlights the accomplishments that have already been made under No Child Left Behind and calls for further expansion of the charter school system. Starting in the 1980s, the charter school movement has called for "schools of choice"—free, public schools that are exempt from certain state and federal regulations that apply to other public schools in exchange for meeting certain standards established in their charter. Supporters of the movement, Spellings included, praise these schools for their increased flexibility and high standard of accountability.

Margaret Spellings's speech: Thank you, Tom Donohue, for introducing me. I'd also like to thank the U.S. Chamber of Commerce for hosting us and Tom Donohue and Art Rothkopf for co-chairing the Chamber's Business Coalition with John Castellani and Susan Traiman. I'd also like to thank the greater business community for leading the charge on workforce readiness.

People like TechNet's Lezlee Westine and NAM's John Engler, who unfortunately couldn't be here today, have made a real difference with NCLB and the President's competitiveness agenda.

I'm happy to be here today to celebrate the 5-year anniversary of *No Child Left Behind* with the people who made the law possible. Since I also just celebrated my fifth wedding anniversary, I've been thinking a lot about what anniversaries mean. And by the way, while wood may be traditional after 5 years, every girl knows that the right gift is always diamonds!

Delivered on January 8, 2007, at Washington, D.C.

Anniversaries also remind us that every day, we have to recommit ourselves to the things that are important to us. And when it comes to education policy, this is a critical moment. With *No Child Left Behind*, we set the goal to have every student reading and doing math on grade level by 2014. And it's working!

- The Nation's Report Card showed our younger students made more reading progress in 5 years than in the previous 28 combined

- Reading and math scores are reaching all-time highs for younger students

Now it's time to renew the law—and I'm counting on your help to get the job done this year. *No Child Left Behind* came about in the first place because people like you recognized that our education system was broken.

Everybody here knows that before this act became law, kids often moved from grade to grade, and nobody knew whether or not they had learned to read, write, add, or subtract. We invested billions of dollars and basically just hoped for the best. The lack of accountability helped create an achievement gap where poor and minority students lagged far behind their peers.

So when President Bush first came to Washington back in 2001, the nation was ready for reform. The President made *No Child Left Behind* his first priority—literally from his first day and his first week in office. And so did members of Congress from both sides of the aisle.

- I remember that first week vividly—every single speech the President gave was about education

- I was present when he and Senator Ted Kennedy met on education for the first time

- Representative Boehner talks about how he thought he was getting the consolation prize when he became Chairman of the House Education and the Workforce Committee—and he also says it became one of the most important accomplishments of his life so far

- Their mutual respect came from the fact that we all knew how much was at stake

Later today, we'll be back in the Oval Office with the President and Congressional leaders to talk about building on the progress we've already made.

- Renewing NCLB is one of the President's top priorities

- I'm confident that Chairman Kennedy, Senator Enzi, Chairman Miller, and Representative McKeon will continue to be strong supporters

- From the start, they've stayed true to the core principles of NCLB—because they know those principles are right and righteous

- I read in the paper recently that Chairman Miller said, "If NCLB is gone, America's poor kids will again be forgotten." And I couldn't agree more.

The business community was key to the passing of the law in 2000, I'm counting on you to play an even greater role this year. I've also been impressed with the personal commitment of several CEOs who I want to mention even though they're not able to be here today, including:

- Craig Barrett (Intel)

- Art Ryan (Prudential)

- Ed Rust (State Farm)

From my point of view, regardless of where you're starting from, active, engaged business communities are key to improving our schools. In states like Massachusetts, Maryland, and California, private sector involvement is making a meaningful difference in students' lives.

That's why it's so important that the Chamber is now supporting reform on a national level. You know better than anybody that our education system has not kept pace with the rising demands of the workplace. So I don't have to tell you that:

- Half of African-American and Hispanic students fail to graduate from high school on time

- Two-thirds of high-growth, high-wage jobs require a college degree, but only a third of Americans have one

- We spend more than a billion dollars each year—and much by you in the business community—on remedial classes for college students who didn't get the education they needed in high school

I'm counting on you to be on the front lines as we head into the process of renewing this law. There are a lot of myths and misconceptions out there, and we must set them straight.

We've heard it all before . . . we're testing too much. We're teaching to the test. We're narrowing the curriculum. The law is unfunded. It's punitive. It unfairly labels schools as "failing." And its goal of having all students on grade level by 2014 is simply not possible.

But as I've traveled around the country, I've met thousands of parents who are grateful to have more information on how their students are doing.

Recently, my Department received an email from Emma Elizalde [el-ee-zal-day], a parent in San Jose, California. She wrote, "Perhaps for some high-level executives from school districts, colleges, and universities, the message about [this law] might take a while to grasp. But . . . for parents, the message came straight to the heart and without delay." As a mother, I know exactly what she means.

Not once in all my travels have I met a parent who didn't want their child learning on grade level now—let alone by 2014. I know I do, and I'm sure every parent in this room agrees.

Of course we know that there are a few students who may need additional time or accommodations to reach grade level—such as those with significant disabilities, or those who have just arrived in our country and are still learning English. And we at the Education Department have already made changes to help states and schools factor that into their measuring systems.

As for testing, I believe President Bush is absolutely right when he says you can't solve a problem unless you diagnose it. If you don't know a child is having a problem, how can you fix it? If you don't measure, how do you know that students are making progress?

To help schools in need of improvement, *No Child Left Behind* provides resources—including free tutoring for struggling students. And President Bush and the Congress have increased federal K–12 spending by 41 percent over the last five years.

- It's not enough to simply ask how much we're spending

- Every year, we have the same conversation about funding at the local, state, and federal levels . . . and we'll have it again this year

- But the most important question is whether students are learning

The truth is, *No Child Left Behind* helps kids by measuring their progress and holding schools accountable for helping them improve. It helps teachers by providing them with information to better manage their classrooms, and resources to improve and enrich their teaching. And it helps businesses by helping students gain the skills they need to succeed.

- I've worked in policymaking for 20 years, and I've yet to see a perfect law—especially one as far-reaching as this one

- But the core principles of NCLB are as strong and sound as they were five years ago

As we move forward with reauthorization, we must preserve these principles while improving the law. I look forward to working with the Congress to get this very important job done.

The next big questions in American education are:

- Are we going to make accountability as meaningful as it should be? Are we going to give schools credit for students' progress over time?

- What will it take to help the students who are struggling the most?

- How are we going to use people and time more effectively to reach the neediest students?

As I said before, I can't imagine a better way to celebrate the fifth anniversary of *No Child Left Behind* than to spend it with all of you. Because I'm counting on you, and the country is counting on you. We've made real progress . . . and we have a lot of important work ahead. Together, we'll succeed.

Thank you, and I'd be happy to take your questions.

Keynote Address to the National Education Association (NEA) Representative Assembly

Reg Weaver

President, National Education Association (NEA), 2002– ; born Harvey, IL, August 13, 1939; B.S., Illinois State University; M.S., Roosevelt University; teacher, Danville High School, Danville, IL; local NEA president, Harvey, IL, 1967–71; president, Illinois Education Association, 1981–87; member, NEA executive committee, 1989–95; vice president, NEA, 1996–2002.

Editor's introduction: The 86th meeting of the NEA Representative Assembly in Philadelphia, PA, featured not only Reg Weaver's keynote address, but also appearances by three candidates for the Democratic presidential nomination—Senators Hillary Clinton, John Edwards, and Chris Dodd. As the 2008 election approaches, Democrats are working hard to court educators, many of whom have expressed frustration with certain provisions of the No Child Left Behind Act. Regarding that law, Weaver states in his address: "The purpose of education is not to score well on standardized tests. The purpose of education is to give young people the tools that they will need to fulfill and satisfy the meaning of learning."

Reg Weaver's Speech: Thank you, and welcome to Philadelphia.

I cannot think of a better place to celebrate our nation's birthday and the 150th anniversary of the National Education Association.

One hundred fifty years ago, this city was in the throes of dramatic change, steamships and railroads were beginning to replace sailing vessels and horse-drawn carriages. The telegraph had recently linked Philadelphia to Washington, D.C. and New York allowing news to travel almost immediately. Immigrants poured into the city to work in factories and mills. And at the same time, a new class of wealthy business titans was rising along with the city's first skyscrapers.

In 1776, Philadelphia had been the cradle of the American revolution. And 30 years later, it was the center of a new revolution, the industrial revolution.

That was the scene in 1857 when 43 educators gathered right here. They were a small group of people, but they had a big idea, the national association to support education and promote its importance in American life. They understood that there was a new revo-

---

Delivered on July 2, 2007, at Philadelphia, PA. Reprinted with permission.

lution, a new revolution underway that would transform our nation and the entire world, and they were determined to be a force for change.

This was the birth of our organization, the National Education Association.

Today, the sailing ships are long gone, and so are the steamships and the telegraph and most of the railroads and many of the factories. The industrial revolution has given way to the information age.

But some things have remained constant. Education has been the most powerful driving force behind all of the changes that have altered our daily lives in so many ways. And the National Education Association is still a dynamic force for change. Only three years, only three years after the organization was born, in 1857, our nation plunged into a bloody civil war, and after the war ended, the fledgling national teachers association took a strong stand for public education for all children, black, and white.

The NTA was only ten years old when it won its first major legislative victory, persuading congress to create the first federal agency for education. The next year, the NTA and several other organizations joined forces to become the National Education Association. And although women were not originally admitted as members, that would soon change, and the NEA would elect its first woman president Ella Flag Young, ten years before women gained the right to vote. NEA was active in the women's suffrage movement as well as the other great social movements of the 20th century: laws to abolish child labor, collective bargaining for workers and legislation to guarantee the civil rights of every American, regardless of race or color or creed. And all along the way, we were the undisputed heavyweight champions for universal public education.

Today, we take it for granted that every child should have an opportunity to get an education, but that right wasn't just handed to us. It was won through hard work of millions of educators who came before us and other people who understood the importance of education and today we are still fighting to make sure every child is afforded a basic right to a good education. In 1938, the NEA published a book titled *The Purpose of Education in American Democracy*. The authors wrote, "There has been a ceaseless struggle for the extension of education to all." A ceaseless struggle.

That struggle continues today in our effort to fulfill our vision of a great public school for every child. The roots of that struggle reach back not only to our beginning 150 years ago, but they reach back almost eight centuries.

As educators, we know it is important to study history. It teaches us from where we have come, how far we have to go, and how far we have come. That is why the NEA is sponsoring an exhibit of historic documents at the National Constitution Center this week. These documents trace the evolution of the values upon which our nation was founded. I hope that you will take the time to visit this remarkable exhibit, which includes an original copy of the Magna Carta, a working draft, and a copy of the Emancipation Proclamation signed by President Lincoln.

The Magna Carta laid the groundwork for our nation's Declaration of Independence which was written right here in Philadelphia. And in the Declaration, Thomas Jefferson wrote that all men are created equal, that they are endowed by their Creator with certain inalienable rights that among them are life, liberty and the pursuit of happiness. The happiness he was referring to wasn't the passing enjoyment or the experience that we get when we watch a funny movie or eat an ice-cream cone. He meant that every human being deserves the opportunity to create a life that provides deep satisfaction, a life that includes some understanding of the world and an appreciation for the beauty of art and nature, a life that allows a person to dream and then to give those dreams the opportunity to be achieved, folks.

This inalienable right can only be enjoyed by people who have an opportunity to get an education. It is not possible to achieve the democracy that Thomas Jefferson envisioned unless every person in our country has that opportunity. And this is why I say that education is the cornerstone of the American dream.

Two hundred years ago, access to a good education was the privilege of a fortunate few. Poor people could not afford to send their children to school, and in many places, it was illegal to teach black kids how to read.

Today we recognize that education should not be a privilege. It is a fundamental right as basic as those rights that were enumerated in the Magna Carta and the Declaration of Independence. The movement for mass education enabled our nation to create the most vibrant economy in history. In the 20th century, delegates, our economy became the envy of the world, not because we had more millionaires than any other nation, but because ordinary people in the United States were able to enjoy a comfortable standard of living, and we achieved that standard of living for one simple reason: because of education.

In 1913, before all states required mandatory school attendance, the average educational attainment of people in the United States was 6.93 years of school, slightly behind Germany and England. By 1989, thanks to the American-led movement for universal high school and the GI bill, our average educational attainment has shot up to 13.9 years. This was the highest level of education in the world, and almost two years more than the second place nation, Japan.

Folks, what do you think happened to the economy between 1913 and 1989? The United States surpassed Europe to become the world's powerhouse. Japan also rose economically as its education levels increased. This was not a coincidence, folks. The economic dominance of the United States in the 20th century was a direct result of universal education which NEA fought hard to achieve.

But what about technology, you ask? What about technology? What about the telephone? What about the radio? The television? Computers, cell phones, the Internet? What about biotechnology and robotics? What about jet airplanes and satellites?

Yep, technology changed our lives, but where did all of this technology come from? It was all invented by individuals who were able to realize their potential because of education. One of the 56 signers of the Declaration of Independence was Philadelphia's own Benjamin Franklin, folks.

Benjamin Franklin knew the importance of education. He said, "Genius without education is like silver in the mine." As educators, it is our job to extract the silver from the mine so that it can shine. Before there is an inventor in a laboratory, there is a child in a classroom, a child who is inspired to learn and to ask questions and to seek and to search for answers to problems.

Our nation has prospered because we took a democratic approach to education. That approach is reflected not only in who we teach, but also in how we teach. In our free society, we value each person as an individual. So we teach students to think for themselves. And that is why the United States has led the world in innovation and technology. That is why our economy has been the envy of the world. And this is why we cannot allow our schools to be judged solely on the basis of one-size-fits-all, multiple-choice tests.

Ladies and gentlemen, even if we meet all of the criteria of No Child Left Behind, it still won't prepare our children for the 21st century. It won't prepare them to compete with children from India and China. It won't give them the skills that they need to think for themselves. And it will not lead to more economic opportunities for our children and grandchildren.

The purpose of education is not to score well on standardized tests. The purpose of education is to give young people the tools that they will need to fulfill and satisfy the meaning of learning. That's the purpose of education: To think for themselves, to solve problems, to pursue happiness. Students from China and Japan and India and Canada and other nations, they come here, folks, they come here in search of academic excellence and diversity.

In 2004, there were approximately 580,000 foreign students enrolled in American colleges and universities. They came here because they know that this is where the greatest minds in the world are working to solve the greatest challenges of the day. We can all take pride. We can all take pride in what our system of public education has accomplished, but you know what, folks, we cannot rest on our laurels, because even today, for millions of our young children, the right to a quality education is still being denied. And until that right is enjoyed by all, we cannot rest. We cannot rest because our way of life and our system of public education are being threatened.

The world is changing rapidly, and we all worry about what the future will hold for our children and grandchildren. And what worries me most, what keeps me awake at night is the danger of losing our ability to compete in a new economy. What was unimaginable a generation ago has begun to occur. Other nations are matching, and in some cases surpassing our educational attainments.

Most of the 50 million children who attend our public schools are getting an excellent education. But folks, most isn't good enough. From the Benton harbor to Los Angeles, from Akron to San Antonio, to Chicago's south side to rural South Carolina, millions of children are caught in a downward spiral of poverty and unemployment and failure in school.

Two of the most significant moments in the history of education, in the history of education in the United States were the Supreme Court's *Brown* decision and the "Little Rock Nine." And both of these events dealt a crushing blow to legal segregation in our public schools. Both promised equal education opportunities for every American child. But today, more than 50 years later, the promise of *Brown* and the legacy of the Little Rock Nine have not been fully realized. And folks, last week's Supreme Court ruling will make it even harder to fulfill the promise of equality in the classroom.

> We cannot overlook the social context that shapes the minds and the hearts of our children and our students.

We are the first organization, I believe, that has met since that decision. I do believe, folks, that we ought to put a call out for the various groups to come together, to see what we are going to do as it relates to the impact of this decision. And we all know about the intolerable achievement gaps in education. Minority and poor children, especially in rural areas and large cities consistently fall behind in basic math and reading skills. It isn't because they can't learn. It's because they never had a real opportunity to learn. From the day they walk into a classroom, these children are at a disadvantage because of the poverty and the unemployment that ravages their homes and their communities. They often don't get enough healthy food to eat or medical care when they need it. And they often don't have anybody at home who has ever read a book to them.

The achievement gaps are not an indictment of their public schools, they are an indictment of the chasms that exist in our larger society, folks. Chasms such as resources. Chasms such as hope. Chasms such as opportunity. It's no wonder that these children are on the wrong side of the chasms, and that they wind up on the wrong side of the achievement gaps.

The so-called No Child Left Behind assumed that schools by themselves could close the achievement gaps, but we can't close the achievement gaps without bridging the other chasms in our society, folks. We cannot overlook the social context that shapes the minds and the hearts of our children and our students. And we know that testing and accountability alone will not close the achievement gaps.

We need programs that actually prepare children to succeed, programs like high quality early childhood education programs. Programs that help parents to become more involved in their children's education. And smaller class sizes, so that every child can get the individual attention that he or she deserves. We need competitive pay, competitive pay, competitive pay! And opportunities for professional development for our educators. We need tutoring and mentoring, and other programs to help children who are at risk before they fall behind. We need a national strategy to keep children in school and reduce the dropout rate.

These programs are not extravagant wishes. They should be basic rights, because without them, millions of our children will never realize their right to a quality education. We have had enough studies on these issues. We have had enough studies. We know that programs like universal pre-K and smaller class sizes will work. The time for talk is over, folks. It is now time for action. It's time for action!

Today we return to the city of Philadelphia, the place of our founding and the cradle of American liberty, to propose an education bill of rights on behalf of children and the United States of America:

- The right to universal preschool and full-day kindergarten.

- The right to small class sizes.

- The right to well-trained and well-paid educators and professionals.

- The right to engaging and challenging curriculums and quality textbooks.

- The right to active participation by parents.

- The right to adequate and equitable funding and other resources for our public schools.

- The right to receive help for English language learners and students with special needs.

- The right to a high school diploma or GED certificate, ensured by graduation requirements, thus reducing the dropout rate.

- The right to equal educational opportunities to ensure that the children achievement gap is closed.

- The right to have multiple measures used to determine student learning because no one ultrahigh-stakes test should determine the future of a child. No one ultrahigh-stakes test should determine the future of a child.

These are rights that guarantee the basic right of every child in our society to a quality education, a basic right that is still being denied to millions of children. Securing these rights will not be easy. There is no magic bullet, and it will take a sustained effort by many people. But we must succeed because we simply can't afford to squander the minds and the talents and the energies of millions of young people.

In the past, economic prosperity was built on an abundance of natural resources or the financial capital needed to create the physical infrastructure. (Now, I want you to stay with me, now.) But in the general economy of the 21st century, economic success will increasingly depend on human capital. And if we want to maintain our standard of living and a place of leadership in the world, we must rise to this challenge.

If we want the best for our children, we must invest in their education. Sadly, that commitment is lacking in our nation today. We are not investing in the human capital that our nation will need to remain strong and prosperous. Today, most states are trying to adapt to a changing economy by offering tax cuts to industries that promise to create jobs—promises that often go unfulfilled. For example, one company got a state subsidy of $270,000 and only created one job at a fast-food restaurant. In Louisiana, oil companies got tax subsidies of a half a million dollars for every new job. And in Florida, one company got a million dollar tax break for every job.

We are placing our economic future, not in the hands of our children, but in big corporations. And across the nation, tax breaks to attract industry cost our states more than $50 billion a year. And federal tax loopholes for businesses cost our nation another $50 billion a year. Now, delegates and the press, these giveaways are handed out with no rhyme or reason and no accountability. And this is the wrong approach, folks. This is the wrong approach. And there is a better way.

The fact is that every dollar that we invest in education will create more jobs than a special tax break for business. Today, on this day, I am calling on the business community of our nation to become our partners in support of public education. I am calling on Congress to close the special tax loopholes that waste resources that we need to invest in our children. And I am calling on all educators to stand together to demand a renewed commitment to development of our nation's human capital.

Now, my question to you is, will you answer the call? Will you answer the call? Will you join me in demanding the kind of national investment that will pay dividends for all Americans and not just to stockholders of favored companies? We don't have to invent the wheel. We don't have to invent the wheel. There is a successful model that we can use, one that will benefit higher education as well as our public schools.

Now, I grew up in the Midwest, and agriculture is very important in that region as it is in most regions. In the Midwest, as in most regions of the country, almost every county has an agricultural extension agent. This person is a valuable resource for every farmer in town. They count on him or her to provide them with advice and assistance. Agricultural agents, in turn, are supported by the experimental stations at land grant universities in every state. The agricultural extension service has worked wonders for the farmers of America.

In 1945, it took up to 14 hours of labor to produce 100-bushels of corn on two acres of land. Forty years later, it took three hours of work and only one acre. A similar program, delegates, a similar program can produce the same kind of results for the entrepreneurs of the 21st century.

It can strengthen our universities and our public schools. And it can develop the human capital that is our nation's greatest strength.

So I call this plan the Extension Service for Knowledge and Information and Development—KIDS.

Now, what I want you to do, I want you to put up on the screen that triangle. Delegates, I want you to look at that triangle. The thing that gets my gall is for the past 25 years, every report that has come forth has come forth with recommendations on only part of the education puzzle. It's only come up with recommendations as it relates to standards assessment and accountability. But the other parts of the puzzle, people don't want to talk about. When you look at that triangle, start at the very bottom, and you will see an economic structure and tax base. That economic structure and tax base leads you to adequate and equitable funding, which leads you to the next layer, which is school system capacity. At the apex of the triangle, you see accountability.

Now, folks, what the people do, they want to hold you accountable, but they never want to give you the economic structure and tax base. They say to you, delegates to the NEA RA, you have to be responsible for all of the outputs or test scores. And you say, I don't mind being held accountable, but give me what I need. So I'm saying to you, delegates, it is now time for us to say that all of the education puzzle has to be talked about, standards, assessment and accountability, but also what we need in order to be successful.

Talk about the economic structure. Talk about the adequate and equitable funding, because if you do not have adequate and equitable funding, you will not have school system capacity.

This proposal that I'm calling for, it calls for closing the federal tax loopholes and strengthening our investment in education at all levels.

Now, under this proposal, states under the federal government will design economic development centers at major universities, and these centers would create research stations to develop innovations in the businesses that will drive the 21st century economy. The knowledge and the expertise from these research centers would then be available at local schools and through local extension agents. A program like this would empower millions of entrepreneurs across the United States to start businesses and create jobs. It would fuel new research in areas like alternative energy, and robotics, and biotechnology. It would strengthen our universities and improve our public schools. This is the kind of commitment to education that our nation needs, the kind of commitment our children and grandchildren deserve. The kind of commitment that reflects the NEA's vision of great public schools for every child.

If Congress and corporate America answer our call, which I know they will, we can have this plan in place by 2010, and within the next decade, we will begin to see the fruits of our investment in our children. We will move closer to fulfilling the education bill of rights. Some businesses will complain about losing special tax breaks, but businesses would benefit most from this plan. Businesses can raise their own financial capital, but they depend on our nation's schools and universities to develop the human capital that they also need. And some politicians might be afraid to support a proposal like this, because it will involve a long-term investment. But when it comes to national security, they don't mind spending money. Now, we have to invest in our economic security. And since the invasion of Iraq four years ago, this war has cost our nation almost one trillion dollars. That's a trillion with a "t." And that is more than the total federal investment in elementary and secondary education programs since ESEA was enacted in 1965, 42 years ago.

So for the sake of comparison, here are some other ways that we could have invested that one trillion dollars:

- We could have hired more than seven million additional teachers for one year.

- We could have paid for almost 50 million children to attend a year of Head Start.

- We could have provided four years of scholarships at public universities for almost 20 million students.

- We could have covered the 55 million Americans who don't have health insurance.

I will leave it up to you to decide whether the war has strengthened our national security. But I believe, I do believe that it has threatened our economic security by draining resources that we should be investing in our children's future.

Our approach to funding education has not changed significantly in at least 30 years. Now that approach must change, and the National Education Association must be a force for change.

We must provide leadership so that our nation can invest in the human capital that we will need to remain strong and prosperous. The NEA is actively working with state and local affiliates to bargain for policies that will close the achievement gap. And we are redoubling our efforts to reach out to ethnic minority communities and organizations and leaders, and we recognize that to achieve a great public school for every child, we must engage these communities on the nation, state and local level, but we won't be able to participate or provide a great public school for every child without adequate and equitable resources and investments.

This is a heavy undertaking. But I know that we are up to the task because we are strong. Fifty years after beginning right here in Philadelphia, we had grown to represent 5,000 educators. On our 100th anniversary, we were 700,000 strong. When you elected me five years ago, we had 2.6 million members. Today, we are 3.2 million across the United States, and we are one of the largest labor organizations in the world. But what makes us special isn't just our size. And it's just not our rich history, of which we are justifiably proud. What makes us special is our purpose.

You didn't join the National Education Association because it was popular. You joined for a purpose. You didn't join because we had a catchy slogan. You joined because we have substance. You didn't join because we fight. You joined because we fight for what is right. We have the numbers. We have the courage. We have the voice. And we have the tide of history on our side, because we are fighting to expand opportunity and equality.

We're fighting in Utah where the Utah Education Association organized a coalition that gathered 124,000 signatures in the first successful petition for a statewide referendum in 33 years. And thanks to this effort, the voters will have a chance to override a bill to create private school vouchers.

We are fighting in Florida where the legislature scrapped Jeb Bush's plan for educator bonus pay in favor of a better program that the FEA helped create.

We are fighting in Missouri where the state house killed Governor Matt Blunt's bill to give tax credits for private school tuition and the state Supreme Court ruled that public employees have a right to bargain collectively.

And we are fighting in Kentucky, where the KEA killed language in two bills that would have handed out powerful bonuses to a handful of educators instead of improving pay for all teachers.

And we are fighting in Connecticut, where the CEA was the driving force behind legislation that will dramatically improve pension funding for state educators while saving taxpayers $2.8 million.

We are fighting in West Virginia, [where we] played a key role in developing legislation that streamlines the grievance processes while protecting the right to judicial appeal.

We are fighting in Washington state, in Iowa, in Minnesota, in Delaware, in Arkansas, where our members helped to pass tough, new laws to protect children and teachers from violence and intimidation in schools.

And all across this country, all across this country, folks, our 3.2 million members are walking in the footsteps of the 43 teachers who gathered here 150 years ago. And we are continuing to wage a ceaseless struggle to expand education opportunities for every child. We are a force for change.

And as we look to the future, we must remain a force for change. Because, my friends, if we are not a force for change, we will be forced to change. There are elements in our nation today who would like nothing more than to use the challenges in our schools as an excuse to destroy the system of public education that has served our nation so well. We cannot—we will not—allow that to happen.

We must do everything in our power to ensure that our children get what they need to succeed in the 21st century, the best education in the world. We must be the driving force for change and reform in education, not mere bystanders. We must be fearless. We must be willing to look for new solutions. We must demand the respect we deserve as professionals who spend our lives on the front lines of education. We must demand a seat at the table every time there is a panel, a seminar, or a discussion on public education.

As educators, our job just doesn't end when the school bell rings. We have to plan tomorrow's meals and drive the children home safely and make sure the buildings are clean and prepare tomorrow's lesson plans. And after all of this is done, we have the responsibility to advocate for the needs of children, and with that responsibility comes a right to be included in policy discussions about education.

So we must insist that our voices are heard. And to ensure that we are not only heard, but heeded, we must engage in the political process that is such a vital part of our great democracy.

Just last week, we saw the importance of the Supreme Court—just one reason why the next presidential election is so important. Just as the English noblemen demanded King John's signature on the Magna Carta, we must demand that candidates for public office acknowledge the basic right of every child to a quality public education. And then we must hold them accountable for taking the necessary steps to secure that right.

In two days, people across the United States will celebrate our nation's birthday. Some will go to the beach. Some are going to go to ball games. Some are going to do cookouts in their backyards and watch fireworks on the town square.

We will have the privilege of celebrating the 4th of July right here in Philadelphia, our nation's birthplace. And no matter how we observe the day, the hearts of all Americans will swell with pride when we think about the great values that have guided our nation.

Today, as I look out over the thousands of educators in this building, my heart is already swelling with pride. It fills me with pride to know that we are part of a profession that has been such a positive force for change. It fills me with pride to know that we have made the world a better place one child at a time. It fills me with pride to know that we will not abandon our ceaseless struggle until every child in the United States has an opportunity to fully share in the American dream.

We have accomplished many things, and today, on our 150th birthday, there ain't no stopping us now, folks. We're on the move. Ain't no stoppin' us now. We got the groove. There's been so many things that held us down, but now, it looks like things are finally coming around. And I know we have a long, long way to go, and where we'll end up, I don't know. But we won't let nothing hold us back. We're putting our show together and we're polishing our act. Well, if you've ever been held down before, I know you refuse to be held down anymore. Folks, ain't no stopping us now from electing a president who is a friend of public education. There ain't no stopping us now from closing the achievement gaps. Ain't no stopping us now from reducing the dropout rate. Ain't no stopping us now from fixing the No Child Left Behind Act.

Thank you for all you do for the children of America. Thank you. Ain't no stopping us now!

II. THE UNITED STATES IN THE GLOBAL MARKETPLACE

The Realities and Rewards of Globalism—Caterpillar's View Toward China

Jim Owens

Chairman and CEO, Caterpillar Inc., 2004– ; Ph.D., economics, North Carolina State University, 1973; corporate economist, Caterpillar Inc., 1972–75; chief economist, Caterpillar Overseas S.A., Geneva, Switzerland, 1975–80; management positions, Accounting, Product Source Planning Departments, Caterpillar Inc., 1980–87; managing director, P.T. Natra Raya, Caterpillar Inc., Indonesia, 1987–90; president, Solar Turbines Inc., Caterpillar Inc., 1990–93; vice president, Group Services Division, Caterpillar Inc., 1993–94; group president, Caterpillar Inc., 1995–2003; vice chairman, Caterpillar Inc., 2003–04.

Editor's introduction: Back in 1984 Caterpillar, the world's leading manufacturer of construction and mining equipment, was facing stiff competition from its Asian counterparts and losing a million dollars a day. By 2006, however, the company earned $40 billion dollars—nearly half of it from abroad. In this address, delivered at the National Manufacturing Week conference, in Rosemont, IL, Owens explains his company's phenomenal turnaround: "Caterpillar is thriving today **not** because we survived globalism, but because we embraced it!" Owens suggests that American manufacturers, instead of hiding behind trade barriers, ought to embrace globalization as an opportunity to make their companies stronger and more efficient.

Jim Owens's speech: Thank you, Governor Engler, and good morning everyone. I'm excited to be here because I believe we have arrived at a critical moment for U.S. manufacturing. I didn't want to miss this opportunity to share my thoughts regarding our industry and our role in an increasingly global economy.

Before I do, let me recognize the NAM for all its work on behalf of manufacturers. Most of that effort comes in Washington, D.C., on the policy front—but they also spend a great deal of time pulling together events like Manufacturing Week. Governor, we thank you and your staff for telling the story of manufacturing in this country.

Delivered on March 22, 2006, at Rosemont, IL. Reprinted with permission.

I'd also like to recognize the Department of Commerce, which has set up an Export Pavilion here, staffed by trade experts from around the world. It's an excellent venue to discuss international business opportunities and a great example of Secretary Gutierrez and the DOC's commitment to American manufacturing.

As Governor Engler said, I have the privilege—and perhaps a little luck—to lead Caterpillar through one of the most exciting and successful periods in our 81-year history. We've just come off our second year of record sales and profits. Our workforce has grown over 20 percent, and our stock price has more than tripled in five years. We've even been getting a little positive press for our performance.

Just last month, *Forbes* printed an article about Caterpillar called "Surviving Globalism." The reporter's main question was this: Cat confronted the same labor costs and Asian competition as the auto companies. But you're doing just fine. Why?

I've been getting that question a lot, and there's no single answer. Some years ago, we began to address rising healthcare costs proactively. We invested substantially in the '80s and '90s to improve productivity and get flexible with our sourcing.

At the same time, we eliminated our centralized, functional structure and established independent business units, each run by a vice president with profit-and-loss responsibility. We stepped up our investment in employee development through Cat University and today spend almost $900 per employee each year. And throughout, we kept our focus on designing high-quality, innovative products that could compete the world over.

The *Forbes* story discussed all these developments. But I think the author buried her lead. Caterpillar is thriving today **not** because we survived globalism, but because we embraced it! And I would suggest that strategy is one the NAM and U.S. business in general must take to heart if we want to continue to be leaders in the global economy.

I come here today with a can-do message. I have the utmost confidence in American manufacturing. My company, Caterpillar, is committed to maintaining a strong North American presence. We want to see all U.S. manufacturers rise to the challenge and take advantage of the opportunity today's global economy presents.

But we have work to do to compete with the world's best. There are steps we must take to get our own house in order. For starters, American manufacturers must focus on designing and producing the highest-quality products incorporating the most up-to-date technology. We have to stay aggressive with our product development programs—and ensure the goods we manufacture are desired the world over.

Second, we must continue to embrace lean manufacturing principles, increase the use of robotics and automation, and focus on just-in-time delivery. These tools will enable us to keep costs low and productivity high.

Third, we must invest in our people—providing the education and workforce development training they need to help us succeed. Over time, our international competitors will work to produce better products and adopt world-class processes—but they cannot replicate our market size and proximity. And the ideas and competitive spirit that our people bring to the workplace must be nurtured.

And fourth, we must believe that we can compete on the world stage. We must look at globalization and international competition as an opportunity to make ourselves stronger and more efficient—and not, as some are proposing, as a reason to turn inward and put up barriers to trade and investment.

I know many of you in the room are small and medium-sized manufacturers who either don't operate globally or do so only on a limited basis—so I won't dwell on Caterpillar's global presence this morning. But I do want to touch on it briefly, because I believe there are lessons to be learned from our experiences.

You know Caterpillar as one of America's major manufacturers. Over the years, we've leveraged our U.S. manufacturing base to become a leading net exporter and major contributor to the health and strength of the U.S economy. Last year alone we exported more than $9 billion in products from the United States.

At the same time, we've also become a major British manufacturer, a major Brazilian manufacturer, and a major Chinese manufacturer—just to name a few of the 40 countries in which we have a presence. We built this footprint throughout the 20th century in anticipation of changing economic conditions and increasing global competition.

In doing so, we discovered that competing against the best international competition makes us a better company. By expanding globally, we have maintained our ability to grow. We refused to concede markets to competitors and thus kept them from gaining undue strength to block our entry. When it made sense to invest for local access, we did so.

In fact, wherever Caterpillar invests, we find that our U.S. exports to these countries increase as well. Take China, for example. Over the last few years, we have more than doubled our Chinese workforce and significantly expanded our sales there. At the same time, we have increased our U.S. exports to China by 40 percent—helping to create some 5,000 new production jobs here in the United States.

Our global footprint also gives us a natural hedge position. History shows that the world's major currencies—dollar, euro, yen—can move anywhere from 15 to 40 percent against one another in a two-year period. In our business, a good margin is 5 to 10 cents on the dollar. Having a fully integrated manufacturing presence in each currency zone helps protect us from these movements.

None of this is to say that operating a global business—particularly with a U.S. manufacturing base—is easy. At Caterpillar, we face many of the same challenges you do. There's the litigation lottery on issues like asbestos—ever-increasing healthcare costs—the lack of a comprehensive energy policy—and I could go on and on.

I am privileged to serve on the President's Manufacturing Council, which includes a cross-section of large, medium, and small companies from across the country and reports through the Department of Commerce. The Council has suggested five areas to focus on to improve American competitiveness.

I don't think I'll get any arguments from you on the first four:

- Tax reform;

- Energy costs;

- Regulatory and healthcare-related costs;

- And innovation and workforce development.

These are issues we must address if U.S. manufacturers are to get on a level playing field with our international competitors. We're all united in our support of policy improvements in these areas, so I won't spend any more time on them today.

Instead, I want to spend the bulk of my time this morning discussing the Manufacturing Council's fifth priority—trade. It's a timely, controversial, and incredibly important issue facing our country today—and one where we have a lot of work to do.

Let's start with the subject everyone is talking about these days—China. Many U.S. manufacturers have made major strides in China over the past few years. We've had to. In Caterpillar's case, China represents a significant portion of the world's sales opportunity for many key products. Economic growth there will almost certainly outpace any other major market.

Unfortunately, the relationship Caterpillar and other companies are building with China is increasingly challenged, primarily by policymakers. They believe U.S. companies can no longer compete on their own and want to isolate America by erecting new trade and investment barriers.

They cite the U.S.–China trade imbalance and what they call "the decline of American manufacturing." Sensing apprehension among many Americans about job security, they increasingly call for protectionist measures and unilateral sanctions.

Attitudes and actions like these trouble me greatly! Let's face it. The United States can no longer go it alone in an increasingly global 21st century economy. We can't operate as a single-engine plane trying to pull the rest of the world along with us. We need a second engine for growth—and China, along with its Asian neighbors, is providing it.

Remember, for a long time the U.S. economy was growing slowly. Europe and Japan were in a funk. And the global economy was performing nowhere near its potential. But now, with the rapid rise of China and India, and the recovery in Southeast Asia, the world economy has begun to boom again. Commodity prices have risen. Global economic growth over the last two years is as strong as most people can ever remember. Hundreds of millions of people have been lifted out of poverty.

And the gains of the Asian economies have not prevented the United States from achieving rapid economic growth and job creation of our own. Inflation and interest rates are low—business confidence is high—and unemployment is very low. Put another way, our economy is hitting on all cylinders.

Yet the general public remains unconvinced. Surveys show they don't trust the President, Congress, or business leaders. And when record U.S. trade deficit numbers were announced in February, protectionists in Congress went into high gear bashing trade—particularly criticizing the U.S. trade imbalance with China.

Instead of focusing on ways to improve U.S. competitiveness, increase American exports, or reverse the steady decline in the U.S. savings rate, many in Congress are pushing for unilateral sanctions—in other words, trade restrictions applied by the United States and not allowed by the World Trade Organization. The most visible example is the Schumer/Graham proposal, which would impose a 27.5 percent tariff on Chinese imports if their government does not address the currency valuation issue. In addition, there are numerous more subtle bills pending that would impose a type of procedural protectionism.

> The gains of the Asian economies have not prevented the United States from achieving rapid economic growth and job creation of our own.

Make no mistake. I strongly believe it is in all of our best interests, including China's, for the Chinese government to revalue its currency—and the sooner, the better. But this anti-China sentiment could be extremely damaging if policymakers on either side of the Pacific make a mistake.

Personally, I can think of no faster path to a worldwide recession than for the twin engines of the global economy—the United States and China—to turn against one another. And if some misguided piece of legislation like the Schumer bill gets through Congress, the chances of that happening are high.

Think about what could result. The United States would import far fewer of China's low-cost products, on which our lowest income citizens depend. The Chinese in turn would import fewer U.S. products and probably slow or stop investing in our treasury bonds. Interest rates would go up. Both economies would spiral downward. And the impact would be felt not just by those of us in business, but by our citizens who can least afford it.

These are the dangers we face if we continue to scapegoat China. While many of our differences are serious, I'm calling on policymakers to pursue a different path—to focus more on "carrots" than on trying to find bigger "sticks." It is time to curb the rhetoric and focus more on engagement. We know that unilateral sanctions rarely work—and in this case would be completely counterproductive.

Instead, let's take actions that encourage China to assume the responsibilities that come with being the world's fourth-largest economy. For starters, China is more likely to address currency and global finance issues if it becomes a full member of the G-8 and takes on a greater role in the International Monetary Fund and other multilateral organizations.

Likewise, China will be more open to cooperate on energy issues if it becomes a member of the International Energy Agency. And it will be more likely to play a much-needed leadership role on world trade if included in the G-6 that provides leadership to the World Trade Organization system.

One of the biggest "carrots" the United States could offer would be to grant China market economy status prior to the 2016 date mandated by the World Trade Organization. Such a change would have important implications regarding how we apply our trade laws toward China—making them more precise and less arbitrary.

But such a change should not even be contemplated unless China is willing to make major changes in how it regulates its economy:

- Far better enforcement of intellectual property protections;

- A continued commitment to fair currency valuation and a meaningful revaluation for openers;

- More transparent institutions;

- And greater reliance on market-based principles.

Would these carrots result in big changes in the way China regulates its economy? Maybe—maybe not. But in our global economy, engagement has a far better track record than unilateral sanctions.

Even though these ideas may not be popular, that doesn't diminish my belief that we have much to lose by trying to bully the Chinese and much to gain by keeping relations positive and constructive. Both countries need to treat one other with mutual respect. Rather than threatening protectionism, leaders must redirect their energies toward improving competitiveness and opening markets.

As my good friend Fred Bergsten at the Institute for International Economics explains, "The future direction of U.S.-China relations will be central to success or failure in resolving the enduring challenges of our time: sustaining global economic growth, alleviating poverty, stemming weapons proliferation, countering terrorism, and confronting new threats of infectious disease and environmental degradation."

In other words, the stakes have never been higher for our country to get China policy right. And it's not just about business success or failure. It's about helping billions of individuals around the world engage constructively in the global economy—helping them gain access to good jobs, good homes, and a better quality of life.

Today we have a new field of entrants to the global stage—not just China, but India, Russia, and the countries of Southeast Asia and Eastern Europe. These new economies are young and fragile.

They need a champion—a leader and a mentor—as they take the important steps toward openness and liberalization. If that champion is not the United States, then who will it be?

Our country has led the charge for trade liberalization since World War II. But today, we're at the point where it takes Herculean efforts to pass a free trade agreement with a small group of Central American and Caribbean countries. We had an even harder time reauthorizing trade negotiating authority for the president.

We—the United States—seem to be on the verge of turning inward! I can't imagine a more disappointing and damaging turn of events—one with profound negative implications for global and U.S. economic prosperity.

Let me share a few statistics. A globalization study by the Institute for International Economics shows that a half century of gradually opening markets has created additional yearly income of $10,000 for the average American household. The Institute's analysis shows that future policy liberalization could add another $5,000 per household per year.

And economic gains aren't the only benefits associated with trade liberalization. Through trade, we raise standards of living. According to the World Bank, the elimination of trade barriers and farm subsidies could lift more than 300 million people out of poverty.

No government aid package can have this kind of impact. And as nations begin to improve their standards of living, they not only engage in the world economy, but are also able to invest in promoting clean air, clean water, and responsible use of natural resources.

That's why trade liberalization is a "win-win-win" proposition. It's good for Caterpillar, it's good for the United States, and it's good for the world!

Now some of you may be saying, "Jim, you run a multinational organization. Of course trade liberalization is good for you. But I'm a small American manufacturer—what's in it for me?"

I'd encourage you to look at it this way: The United States has only 5 percent of the world's population. That means 95 percent of potential customers are located outside this country. As the studies I've just cited prove, trade liberalization brings more and more of these people into the global economy. As their quality of life improves, they become potential consumers of the products you provide.

If the United States adopts trade barriers, however, then all U.S. manufacturers—large and small alike—will see access to these prospective customers restricted.

Unfortunately, we're not hearing rational arguments for trade and against protectionism in our country. Why are there so few pro-trade Democrats? Isn't this the party of John Kennedy and Bill Clinton? Why are so many Republicans starting to look inward? And why aren't more corporate leaders speaking out? It's time to tone down the politically charged rhetoric and embrace a more bipartisan trade policy based on our long-term national interests!

Caterpillar is encouraged by President Bush's pro-trade remarks in India last month, and pleased that he is willing to fight for a more open and liberal trade and investment environment. I also want to acknowledge the leadership of Speaker Denny Hastert. Against seemingly impossible odds, he continues to press for open markets and improved competitiveness.

> It's time to tone down the politically charged rhetoric and embrace a more bipartisan trade policy based on our long-term national interests!

Why? Because he knows, as I do, that only countries not creative enough to compete turn inward—which is certainly not the case with America. Our country has demonstrated over the years that we are resilient. We operate within a vibrant, market-based economy. We know how to determine what our customers want and need. And we have the innovative people who can design and build products to compete in the world market.

This is why I believe so strongly that American manufacturing can win on the world stage. But to do so, we need to focus on putting our own house in order—not on scapegoating China and promoting protectionist policies. And when one of our industries is not competitive in the global economy, we need to do a much better job of helping workers and communities retrain and retool for the future.

The NAM has it right. Your organization understands the power of collaboration, and I've seen it accomplish great things when its members rally around common goals. Today, we are united behind the need to make American manufacturing more competitive. We agree on many of the policy changes we want to see in Washington. Now, it's time that we come together as the lead sector of the U.S. economy to embrace the one issue that presents both the biggest challenges and the greatest opportunities for our success—globalization.

It isn't easy. To quote Thomas Freedman, author of *The World Is Flat*, "If globalization were a sport, it would be a 100-meter dash, over and over and over. And no matter how many times you win, you have to race again the next day."

We at Caterpillar want to stay in that race. We want to win it. And I know all of you gathered here today do, too. It's that spirit of optimism and fierce competitiveness that has made American manufacturing great—and will ensure we stay on top of the world economy for years to come.

With that, let me say thank you. Like you, I'm proud to be in manufacturing, and it's been an honor to speak at Manufacturing Week. I hope my comments today have given you a fresh perspective on competing—and winning—in the global marketplace. I'd be happy to spend the rest of the hour answering any questions you have.

Asia and the Emerging Global Financial System

Lawrence Summers

Charles W. Eliot University Professor, Harvard University, 2006– ; born New Haven, CT, November 30, 1954; S.B., Massachusetts Institute of Technology (MIT), 1975; associate head tutor, Department of Economics, Harvard University, 1978–79; assistant professor, Department of Economics, MIT, 1979–82; Ph.D., Harvard University, 1982; associate professor of economics, MIT, 1982; domestic policy economist, President's Council of Economic Advisers, 1982–83; professor of economics, Harvard University, 1983–87; Nathaniel Ropes Professor of Political Economy, Harvard University, 1987–91; vice president of development economics and chief economist, World Bank, 1991–93; undersecretary for international affairs, U.S. Department of the Treasury, 1993–95; deputy secretary, U.S. Department of the Treasury, 1995–99; U.S. secretary of the treasury, 1999–2001; Arthur Okun Distinguished Fellow in Economics, Globalization, and Governance, The Brookings Institution, 2001; president, Harvard University, 2001–06.

Editor's introduction: With his controversial tenure as president of Harvard University behind him, Lawrence Summers has reemerged as one of the leading voices on economic affairs in the United States. Indeed, "His views on the importance of Asia's growth, the challenges of globalization and the danger of the United States' huge trade deficit are widely promoted by policy makers and economists," according to Heather Timmons for the *New York Times* (April 19, 2007). In this particular speech, delivered at the Asia Society Hong Kong Center Annual Dinner in Hong Kong, China, Summers posits that when history is written 300 years from now, the primary story will not be the end of the Cold War or September 11th, but the rise of Asia as an economic superpower.

Lawrence Summers's speech: It wasn't so long ago that I was introduced by a guy who said, "Larry, do you know what it takes to succeed as an economist?", and I said, "No." And he said, "an economist is someone who's pretty good with figures but does not quite have the personality to be an accountant." That was in Moscow and no one got the joke. Everybody would get the joke in Hong Kong and that's got to say something about what's happening in this part of the world.

It's good to be here with so many old friends and it is good to be here for the Annual Dinner of the Asia Society, which is the kind of organization that I believe is profoundly important in the kind of connections, not just government to government, but citizen to citi-

---

Delivered on September 19, 2006, at Hong Kong, China. Reprinted with permission.

zen, businessperson to businessperson, cultural organization to cultural organization, that are going to be made, that are critical, if transformations underway in the world are to be well-managed. So I am deeply honored by the invitation to speak here.

I come here from Singapore where I attended, for the first time in half a dozen years, the annual IMF/World Bank meetings, and the nature of the discussions at the meetings were quite different than any that I remembered.

Unlike many of the meetings that I remembered, Asia was at the centre of the conversation. Unlike the discussions that I remembered, where Asia was at the centre of the conversation, like those held in 1997 and those held in 1998, the topic was not how we could assure that there was a flow of capital from the industrial world to Asia. It was not about how we could contain a crisis in Asia, it was very much about the flow of capital from the emerging markets of Asia, to the industrial world. It was not about the challenge that Asia posed, but about the opportunity that it represented. It was about Asia as a source of savings as well as a locale for investment.

Tonight, what I'd like to do is reflect on Asia's rise with China at the centre of the story. Initially, in a broader historical perspective and then, in the medium term to focus in particular, on the global financial challenge that are posed and posed especially, by the magnitude of current global imbalances.

Begin with this: economic developments in Asia, in the past generation and especially in China, are without precedent in human history and are of profound historical importance.

They called it the Industrial Revolution because after 2000 years, when growth proceeded at rates where it was barely noticeable and all of a sudden, something that was then remarkable took place and it became the case that over a human lifespan of that period, 40 or 45 years, a person could expect to see living standards increase by as much as 50 or 75 per cent. So they called that the "Industrial Revolution." Subsequently, in the most rapid phase of economic growth in the United States, in the late 19th century, growth proceeded at a rate where a person could expect, over a human lifespan, to see living standards increase perhaps by as much as four fold. And the world had never seen anything like that.

At a growth rate of 6 to 7 per cent in per capita terms, which is below the growth rate that China has enjoyed in recent years, which is modestly below the growth rates that the newly industrialized economies have enjoyed, living standards will increase by a factor of about 100 in a 75-year human lifespan. A third of humanity is now living in societies where living standards, in a single human lifespan, rise by a factor of 100. Nothing like that has ever happened before.

I would dare to suggest that when the history of this period is written 300 years from now, the end of the Cold War will not, be the primary story. September 11th, Iraq and all that surrounds them, will not be the first story. Rather, the first story will be the rise of Asia and all that it meant for people in Asia and all that it meant for the world system.

Now to be sure, as the prospectuses have it, past performance is no guarantee of future returns. And yet—and there can be no certainties—and yet I think it bears quite considerable emphasis that as the IMF's recent outlook suggests, the level of income today in China is roughly comparable to the level of income in 1967 in the newly industrialized economies when their take-off is said to have begun. And it is roughly comparable to the level of income in Japan in 1955 when its level of income began to rise.

And so while growth has been going on for a long time at a rapid rate, it would be a serious mistake to suppose that with income standards at about 15 per cent of American living standards, that there was not very substantial room for continued rapid growth. And in India, where living standards are approximately half of Chinese living standards, there is even more room for rapid growth.

> The first story will be the rise of Asia and all that it meant for people in Asia and all that it meant for the world system.

And so I would say to you that this phenomenon that you all are part of, that the whole world is part of, really does rank, in the last millennium, only with the Renaissance and the Industrial Revolution in terms of its ultimate historical significance.

Changes of this magnitude do not happen without profound consequences. And how those consequences are managed in every sphere by the countries involved and by the other countries that are influential in the world system, principally my country, will, I believe, define the history of this next century.

It is one of the lesser, but not insignificant, aspects of the period following September 11th that these matters, which would otherwise be top of mind for U.S. policymakers and for Americans more generally, have not, in my view, received the careful attention that they deserve.

As we reflect in the international community on all that will be meant by Asia's rise, we need, I believe, to recognize, as is insufficiently recognized in much of the Western discussion, that just as we shape our destiny, Asia's destiny will be shaped in Asia.

With 700 million people still in extreme poverty, with growth at these rates transforming almost every aspect of societal life, from increased urbanization to changed patterns of regional equality and inequality, to changes in traditional patterns of social mobility. With the inevitable consequences and political pressures and political strains that come with the emancipation represented by standards of living that double every decade or less, it is inevitable that the pre-occupation of governments in Asia will be with what all of this means for their citizens and for their societies rather than primarily, what it means for the international community.

The United States and Europe and the rest of the world, have an enormous stake in how this progress takes place, on how China, India and the other countries in Asia define their greatness during their renaissance.

I would suggest, as a general principle that applies well in all areas, that policymakers from the West would do well to speak with their Asian colleagues in the interrogative rather than the imperative form because there is an enormous amount that we have to understand if we are going to constructively engage.

Now there are many spheres in which Asia's growth will have profound global consequences. It will have enormous consequences for the balance of power for the global security order. It will have profound consequences for the global energy market and profound consequences for the global environment.

I will leave these topics aside. I want to focus on what it will mean for the global economy and in particular the challenge of maintaining sustainable growth and integration.

To be sure, growth with integration is no guarantee of stability. Western Europe, between 1905 and 1914, had plenty of growth and plenty of economic integration. But, if integration is no guarantee of stability, I would suggest to you that disintegration and the failure of sustained and integrated growth virtually guarantees insecurity and instability.

Let me speak frankly. I am deeply concerned about the medium term sustainability of the current global economic patterns connecting the emerging markets of Asia and the United States. While, as I shall suggest, these patterns are both beneficial and functional on both sides of the Pacific in the short run, that very short run constructive aspect has a tendency to blind policymakers to the medium-term challenge of sustainability that they represent.

What am I talking about? I am talking about the following: the United States is now running a current account deficit of between 6 and 7 per cent of GNP with the magnitude of that current account deficit increasing rather than decreasing. According to the IMF's projection, the US current account deficit will approach $1 trillion next year.

What does it mean to say that the United States is running a current account deficit? It means a number of things that economics courses teach are essentially identical. It means that we're importing a trillion dollars more than we're exporting. It means that we're spending a trillion dollars more than we're earning. It means that we're investing a trillion dollars more than we're saving.

There is no economic theory that suggests—[mobile phone rings]— that tune is sort of vaguely reassuring in the midst of all of this. There is no economic theory that suggests that borrowing a trillion dollars at an increasing rate is a permanently sustainable strategy.

Now to be sure, there is always the argument that is made—and it's a standard one that every Treasury Secretary or Finance Minister of a country with a substantial current account deficit has always made—that can be put this way: wouldn't you rather live in a country that capital was trying to get into than a country that capital was trying to get out of? And so isn't it terrific that a trillion dollars of capital wants to get in to the United States?

Maybe. And certainly the much smaller current account deficits that we had in the 1990s could be linked very clearly to increased capital formation and increased physical investment in American plant and equipment.

The data speak unambiguously to the current account deficit that the United States is now running. It is financing consumption. Savings has collapsed in the last five years, spurred primarily by increased budget deficits and despite the widening current account deficit, investment has declined rather than increased.

Indeed if one looks at the path of foreign direct investment or one looks at investments in equity, the United States is a net exporter of long-term capital rather than a net importer of long-term capital.

I suspect you know what's coming next: what is the source of this finance? The source of this finance is, for the most part, not the decisions of individual private investors deciding where it is most profitable for them to locate their capital. US current account deficits are largely mirrored by increases in reserve assets that reflect choices of governments around the world with the most important of those governments being the government of China and more generally, the governments of East Asia.

That capital is being acquired out of an entirely appropriate—indeed when I was at the Treasury I advised it—desire to accumulate reserves so as to prevent financial instability and to insure against any possible recurrence of the Asian Financial Crisis of the late 1990s.

The level of reserves in China, which now approach a trillion dollars, in the developing world generally, which now approach 2½ trillion dollars, are far beyond any measure of what is needed to ensure stability. Indeed they represent approximately five times the level of all debts coming due within the next year. Rather, the accumulation of reserves comes not out of a strategy of accumulating reserves, but as a by-product of a strategy of maintaining exchange rates at very competitive levels that support export led growth.

This alignment is very functional in the short run. Americans get to spend more than they earn, and to finance that spending, at very low rates—4 to 5 per cent in nominal terms. After correcting for inflation, 1 to 2 per cent in real terms. The suppliers of capital to the United States are not earning a very high return on their lending—the same 1 or 2 per cent at best. But they are supporting a level of export demand that provides a very strong impetus to growth. And so growth in the capital supplying countries, who might be said to be engaged in a kind of vendor finance for their exporters, the ability to keep spending in the United States, is a short-term, very healthy dynamic.

But I would suggest to you that in the medium term, it is unsustainable for three reasons, any one of which is sufficient to bring it to an end at some point.

First, it can't be the case that any country can be allowed to increase the magnitude of its debts at an indefinite rate forever. And so borrowing by the United States on this scale is not something that will be indefinitely permitted, nor at a certain point, even if the markets were prepared to do it, will the set of assets that the United States is prepared to sell to foreigners who want to accumulate claims on the United States diminish. Already well over half of the participation at US debt auctions comes from abroad, principally from emerging Asia.

So at the first level, the borrowing is unsustainable. At the second level, the lending is unsustainable because what is it that is driving the lending? It is, you'll recall, the fixing of the exchange rate and the associated accumulation of reserves.

In economic lingo, the difficulty is that those capital inflows cannot be sterilized forever. In regular language, if you keep printing money to buy dollars, eventually you're going to have more and more inflation—first in asset markets and then in product markets. The longer you hold the exchange rate down and the further you hold it from its natural level, the more capital will flow in hoping to be there the day that the exchange rate adjusts. The more you try to raise interest rates in an effort to cool down the economy amidst that inflation, the more capital flows in because the interest rate rises. The more open the financial system becomes, either as a consequence of financial reforms or as a consequence of the general greater integration with the global economy, the more these problems are presented.

Japan's experience in the 1980s is highly suggestive in this regard. It was a rapidly growing economy. It was an exchange–rate oriented economy. It attempted, in the late 1980s, to prevent excessive yen appreciation through monetary policy. The results were enormous asset price inflation—the bubble of the late 1980s that eventually led to the very difficult period of the 1990s.

So you can't forever borrow at these magnitudes and you can't forever lend at these magnitudes. Those are matters of arithmetic. They are matters of hard economics.

The third reason why this pattern is, I believe, unsustainable in the long run, is not a matter of economics or arithmetic, it is a matter of politics. And that is that the concomitant, indeed the very motivation for this whole alignment, is the very substantial increase in US imports relative to US exports or conversely, in the exports of the emerging countries, relative to the imports of the emerging countries. That is terrific for the people who get to produce and it is terrific for the people who get to consume. It is not so good for the people who compete with the people who get to produce. And experience, again and again around the world, suggests that when trade deficits become substantial and sustained, there is very substantial protectionist pressure that results.

It was there in the 1980s when Toyotas were being bashed on the steps of the US capital and it gives me no pleasure to say that protectionist pressures are very substantially increasing, right now, in the United States and Europe. When those protectionist pressures will lead to the taking of precipitous action is not a judgment that I can make. Already, the commitment to free trade and to global integration in the United States and Europe has been substantially attenuated as workers contemplate the implications, for them, of a huge increase in the effective global labor force as Asia rises and technology permits increased integration. There is no surer way to increase protectionist pressures than to increase the magnitude of trade imbalances.

> There is no surer way to increase protectionist pressures than to increase the magnitude of trade imbalances.

Now one could argue or cavil with each of these three points, the question of how long borrowing can take place, the question of how long lending can take place without macroeconomic consequences, and the question of how long the configuration can be maintained without a prophecy–destroying protectionist backlash. But I would suggest to you the odds that all three of those risks can be maintained for five to ten years are very, very small indeed. To be sure, there is no reason for precipitous alarm. The investors who are holding the treasury bills are not the kind of private investors who can panic. They are large actors who will find it very expensive to panic and very damaging to their own economies to panic.

At the same time, the medium-term situation is not sustainable. Nor are there any self-correcting trends in place. The deficit is increasing. The rate of reserve accumulation is increasing. Protectionist pressures are rising. If the situation is not managed, and if it manages itself at some point, either because lenders are unwilling to lend or because borrowers are unwilling to borrow or because speculators decide on a massive scale to speculate against the sustainability of the configuration, the consequences are likely to be very severe.

At the same time, you are likely to see very substantial financial pressure on the US economy as the dollar falls and the supply of credit dries up. And you are likely to see very substantial pressure towards recession in the United States. You also would have the need for painful adjustment in the countries that have been relying on US demand as a source of demand for their exports. Substantial economic disruption in the international system at a time of such tectonic changes obviously carries with it enormous risks.

What then should be done? I would suggest five steps.

First, these are serious issues that need to be addressed but this is not an emergency that requires panic. There is a kind of co-dependency built in from the simultaneous desire to borrow and to lend.

Second, this is the international financial challenge of the next decade and so the fora for international discussion need to assure close working relationships that build trust between the major capital supplying and the major borrowing countries.

The G7, which contains two North American countries, four European countries and Japan and does not include a representative of emerging Asia or a representative of the oil exporting countries, is hardly a suitable group for discussion of these issues. The G20 that was instituted some years ago is a very valuable forum, but a meeting of 20 countries, each of which is represented by a Finance Minister and a Central Bank Governor, is a meeting of 40 people and serious work is not done in meetings of 40 people. And so the design of a process where the management of these issues can be discussed, in a serious way, that builds trust, needs to be established before, rather than after, the crisis.

> *Any solution to global imbalances must start with a US commitment to increased national savings, starting with actions to reduce the budget deficit.*

Third, United States needs to recognize, clearly and explicitly, and act on the recognition that the US trade deficit is made in Washington. It is not made in Tokyo or Beijing or London or Paris. As long as the US net national savings rate—that is the rate at which households save plus corporations retain earnings, less the amount the Government borrows—as long as that number is as it currently is—close to zero, there is no way that the United States can invest to provide for growth without very substantial reliance on foreign borrowing. Any solution to global imbalances must start with a US commitment to increased national savings, starting with actions to reduce the budget deficit and extending to actions to improve household savings. Without such actions, durable solutions that increase the sustainability of the global expansion are not possible.

Next, US increases in savings that reduce the American need to borrow from abroad, without complementary policy action, risk global recession. Why? An increase in US savings reduces the level of US demand, an increase in US savings reduces the level of US interest rates tending to make the dollar less attractive, tending to lead to a Dollar decline, tending to make US goods cheaper and foreign goods more expensive, switching demand from the rest of the world towards the United States.

An increase in US savings without other policy action is a prescription for a slowdown globally. Indeed, when the concern is expressed in debates about this moment, about the consequences of a falling US housing market for the global economy, it is exactly that concern that is paramount. And so, if US savings are to be increased, as they must, there must be complementary measures to increase global demand.

There are many potential sources for such measures. It is not easy though to make the argument that either Europe or Japan has room to substantially increase consumption, relative to their incomes. If anything, the pressures with societies that are aging very substantially operate in the other direction. There is perhaps some scope for increased investment, particularly if appropriate deregulatory actions are taken. But the consequences of those deregulatory measures for the global supply/demand balance are not clear. The largest scope for increasing demand lies within the countries of Asia.

In China, private consumption is approximately 42 per cent of income and it is declining. With the rapid growth that China has achieved, there is very substantial room—and very substantial gains I would suggest—to enabling increased consumption. However, it's very difficult for someone from the outside to prescribe.

One approach that's been suggested is very substantial improvements in social insurance and pension arrangements. So individuals don't have to save so much on a precautionary basis. Another is changing policies on state-owned enterprises to promote the payment of dividends and so reduce corporate savings and, at the same time, reduce the pressure to reinvest free cash flow in relatively unproductive kinds of capital.

These may or may not be appropriate ways to think about moving to a strategy of consumption led growth. But the basic truth is that a large and growing region cannot enjoy export-led growth at an increasing rate without a part of the world that's going to enjoy import led growth at an increasing rate. And the United States cannot afford that. And so, one part of the desirable adjustment process is an orientation towards consumption-led growth. The financial counterpart of that adjustment is moving over time, a process that has begun, towards increased exchange rate flexibility.

Now there's much discussion of the question of the sequencing and the pacing of financial liberalization and exchange rate flexibility. I would suggest that the logic points very much towards exchange rate flexibility preceding financial liberalization precisely because, in the absence of such financial liberalization, the magnitude of capital flows is lower and the controllability of exchange rate fluctuations is, therefore, greater. And so increased exchange rate flexibility will permit the use of monetary policy to provide for economic stability, rather than commit monetary policy to the exchange rate objective, is the other part of a path that is likely to be desirable if these balances are going to be reduced over time.

What will the magnitude of the exchange rate adjustment be? It's very difficult to know. You know it's precisely because it's very difficult to know that economists increasingly recognize and countries increasingly follow the advice that major large economies should have flexible exchange rates because if you have flexible exchange rates, you don't have to know what the right exchange rate is. The market makes the choice.

I would suggest one relevant, overarching lesson of the financial history of the last half-century. There are literally dozens of examples of countries that maintained fixed exchange rates or quasi-fixed exchange rates for too long and then were forced to exit them in a disorderly way or found the consequences of their exit to be wrenching. I know of no example of a country that suffered substantially from the premature movement towards increased exchange rate flexibility. Don't panic, provide fora for trusted discussions, move towards increased savings in the United States, a consumption led growth strategy in emerging Asia.

The fifth thing that I believe is necessary and that I believe represents the reason why gatherings like this are so important, is for the leadership in both countries, on both sides of the Pacific, to do two things that are very difficult in a political context.

> We all have an obligation to do what we can to assure that with all the change, there is a commitment to maintaining as much stability as we possibly can.

The first is to look beyond the moment, to look to problems that are not the problems of today but will be the problems of tomorrow and to take steps that are painful. Increasing savings in the United States through reducing our budget deficit is painful. Starting to make the changes in an enormously complex structure in China that are necessary to move towards consumption led growth does involve consequences that are painful in the short run. And so it does take courage and it does take support to do the painful when it is most effective but not yet obligatory.

The other part of what is necessary on the part of leaders—and by leaders I don't just mean government leaders, I mean those in all kinds of leadership positions in society—is to recognize that it is terribly important to recognize the need for mutuality and to not seek popularity by scapegoating the other side. For us in the United States, not to blame our trade deficit, which results fundamentally from our low level of savings, on the policies of other countries and for those on this side of the Pacific to recognize that they have a stake in the management of these imbalances as well.

In many ways it is this last question, the maintenance of a constructive spirit in addressing a problem before it is imminent and pressing, that is most difficult. It may be that others will believe that some aspects of the analysis I've presented here aren't right but if the broad thrust, that there are questions of sustainability, questions of sustainability that are hidden by the very comfort of these patterns in the short run is right, then a constructive spirit of mutuality on both sides is of profound importance.

Let me finish where I started. What is taking place in Asia is the most important thing that's going to happen in any of our lifetimes. It's the thing that's happening in our lifetimes, in anybody's lifetime, that's creating more human betterment, more human emancipation, more opportunity than anything that's ever happened. We all have an obligation to do what we can to assure that with all the change, there is a commitment to maintaining as much stability as we possibly can and that's why I've chosen tonight to sound this warning.

Thank you very much.

Remarks at the Detroit Economic Club

Mitt Romney

Candidate for 2008 Republican presidential nomination, 2006– ; born Detroit, MI, March 28, 1947; B.A., Brigham Young University, 1971; M.B.A., Harvard University, 1975; J.D., Harvard Law School, 1975; consultant, Boston Consulting Group, 1975–77; consultant, Bain & Co., Boston, 1977–78; vice president, Bain & Co., Boston, 1978–84; managing partner and CEO, Bain Capital, Inc., Boston, 1984–2001; chairman and CEO, Bain & Co., Boston, 1991–2001; president and CEO, Salt Lake Organizing Committee (Winter Olympics), Utah, 1999–2002; governor (R), Massachusetts, 2003–2007.

Editor's introduction: Like many other candidates for the Republican presidential nomination, former Massachusetts governor Mitt Romney supports free trade and has made tax reform a cornerstone of his campaign. In this speech, delivered to the Detroit Economic Club, he argues that tax relief—in combination with low inflation and deregulation—is essential to creating an economic renaissance in the United States. According to Romney, globalization can be a boon for Americans as long as the country makes necessary changes in domestic policy—reforms that hold true to its history of free-market enterprise. He also argues that economic prosperity should be shared, because "economic success that's only narrowly shared will divide a nation ultimately and kill the entrepreneurial spirit and opportunity to pursue happiness."

Mitt Romney's speech: Quite an introduction.

I must admit—I love exaggeration and hyperbole when it applies to me and I, I appreciate that very, very much.

We used to drive Ramblers—I had the Rambler Station Wagon for my dates. My friends called it "Mrs. Romney's Grocery Getter."

I used to ask my dad, "How in the world can you compete as head of America Motors when you've got such huge competitors, GM, Ford, Chrysler, the big three—how do you possibly think you can succeed?" And he'd say in a way that I have not forgotten: "Mitt, there's nothing as vulnerable as entrenched success. There's nothing as vulnerable as entrenched success."

And over the years, we've seen companies that have become complacent and they get passed by nimble upstarts. Big steel was overtaken by the mini mills, the main line air carriers are seeing a real run for their money from people like Jet Blue and Southwest, and

---

Delivered on February 7, 2007, at Detroit, Michigan. Reprinted with permission.

perhaps the most interesting of these cases comes from the computer industry, where IBM was overtaken by Digital and in mini-computers, and then Digital was overtaken by Wang in work stations, and then Wang was overtaken by Compaq in desktops, then, of course, a new distribution model from Dell took over Compaq, and then now you've got HP making another run at, at Dell. It's extraordinary to see what happens.

But there are many companies that are able to maintain their lead, over many, many years. And these are the ones that remain vigilant, that change as their industry faces Speeches challenges. Names like GE, and Hewlett Packard, Microsoft, Motorola come to mind.

The same can be true for countries.

About 100 years ago, at the Golden Jubilee of Queen Victoria, I'm sure people in the audience could not have imagined that any country would ever overtake Great Britain as the world's economic and military superpower. But 50 years later, we had.

It's inconceivable to us today that we could in any way be passed by any other nation. We've been competing with Europe so long that we've gotten a little over-confident. But look east. Asia is emerging as an economic powerhouse. And that's great news: People who couldn't buy our products in the past are now able to buy our goods and services—I must admit, I was delighted in December when I was over in Beijing to see so many Buicks driving around town. But it's also a real challenge as they emerge out of poverty. Will Rogers used to say, "Even if you're on the right track, if you don't move, you'll get run over."

So standing still isn't a viable option for America. The question for us is this: what direction should we take?

History can be a guide for us. The 20th century saw two economic systems pitted against each other. Ours was built on free enterprise and the preeminence of the consumer. The Soviet Union's was built on government control and command, and the preeminence of the state.

Ours produced the most powerful economy in the world and it gave its citizens a standard of living our grandparents would have never dreamed possible; theirs produced a downward spiral standard of living and a collapsed economy.

That 20th century history lesson is what has made us understand why America's economy is so strong and that is because we put our trust in the American people, and in the free enterprises the free American people create.

I spent some 25 years, as John indicated, working in the private economy, starting businesses, acquiring businesses, consulting to businesses, managing businesses. I've invested in companies in Germany, Italy and New Zealand. I've negotiated in China and Ecuador. I've managed businesses in Japan and Russia. You get a lot better in educating yourself by being in the arena than you do by sitting in the bleachers. My successes and failures, by the way, have given me some insights on what I think it takes to grow a business, and an economy, and a nation.

And today, I'd like to offer a few perspectives.

Let me begin with our objectives. On the screen, I hope you can read that, well, maybe you can, maybe you can't; it's a long way away. I'm going to read them. Objective:

Remain an Economic Superpower—we can't be a military super-power unless we're also an economic superpower.

A Growing Economy—growth is essential if you want to have a future that's brighter than your past.

Shared Prosperity—economic success that's only narrowly shared will divide a nation ultimately and kill the entrepreneurial spirit and opportunity to pursue happiness. That's the quintessential American hope and dream—that every person has the opportunity to achieve the success that they desire in their own heart.

Now, the words may sound a little academic there, but don't forget these objectives are very critical to human interests, a higher stan-dard of living, greater job security, a brighter future for our children and income security for our senior years.

Now my experience has taught me that there are a lot of things that create a growing economy and a vibrant nation. Let me look at five of them in particular. Next slide, please.

- Skilled and educated and motivated people, on the top of my list.

- Free Trade, on the Level

- Capital and Savings

- Innovation and Technology

- Consumer Freedom

But, in addition to the things which propel the growth of an econ-omy and create a higher standard of living for our citizens are those things which put in a braking action. On the other side of this equa-tion, next slide, are these five:

- Excessive Taxation and Spending

- Excessive Regulation

- Excessive Burdens on Business Activity

- Excessive Health Care Costs

- Excessive Energy Costs

Now, part of the history of America can be seen by looking at that slide—we've done very well educating our people, making sure they have the skills they need to compete, making sure we have open markets that we can participate in, having adequate capital, assur-ing that we have the leading edge in innovation and technology and relying on the consumer to point the way. We've also done our very best to hold down taxation—John F. Kennedy did that, Ronald Reagan did that, George W. Bush did that. We tried to pare back government regulation when we can. We've also tried to take off burdens on our business activity to hold down our energy costs, and as a result, we've had a vibrant, fast-growing economy over these last 30 years.

Now, you'll be relieved to hear that I'm not going to dwell on every single one of those ten today in great depth, but I want to give you a few thoughts about a number of them.

Let me begin on the one on the far left, which is education. Our schools are falling behind those of other nations—you've seen that. It's true particularly in math and science. Our 15 years olds ranked 24th out of 29 OECD nations in math. 24th out of 29. Our high school seniors rank in the bottom 10% in math and the bottom 25% in science. How can you lead the world if the kids in the next generation are falling behind in the skills they need to innovate and create new enterprises?

Now, when I became governor, I sat down with educators and leaders and said, "What do I have to do to improve our schools?" And some folks said to me, "Well, you have to get a much smaller classroom size. That's key." Coming from the private sector, I don't just take people's advice, I ask for the data. We have 351 cities and towns in Massachusetts. I said, "Let's do something, let's compare the average classroom size of all of our school districts with our performance of the young people on our statewide exams." Because we have statewide exams that determine how well our kids are doing. The chart we expected would have the trend you see in the next slide.

That is, on the bottom, you have the classroom size, from the large classes on the far right-hand side to smaller classes on the left. And then we had how well our schools—our students—were performing. High performers on the top, low performers on the bottom. If there's a strong relationship between how big your classrooms are and how well the kids are doing, there should be a pattern along that line you see—a downward sloping line.

But here's the real data: you can see those red dots, you can see there's no relationship at all. As a matter of fact, some of the districts that had the smallest classes had the worst performance on the student scores. And vice versa. And so we decided to spend a little more time talking to teachers and parents and people who'd focused on education—educators and others. And they came up with a list of things that would really make a difference in education. Let me show you some of those.

First, was making sure that we treated teaching as a profession—not just as a labor job, an hourly labor job. We wanted to make sure that we gave bonuses to our teachers for having math and science capability and AP credentials. We wanted to have bonuses for superior work. We wanted to make sure that we could provide incentives for higher academic achievement. As a matter of fact, we put into place in our state a scholarship called the Adams Scholarship—you score in the top quarter of your high school class on your state exam and you're entitled to 4 years tuition-free at our state universities or state colleges. And so those were the kinds of commitments we made. We also said, "If you want to improve schools, give every kid a laptop computer, make sure that we also have math and science academies where our best and brightest kids can go."

English immersion: we put this in place in our state, no more bilingual education. We said if you want to be successful in a nation that speaks English, you've got to be fluent in English. We also felt it was critical to measure student performance, put in place a graduation exam; we insisted on school choice, longer school days, parental involvement. Parental involvement means not only a preparatory effort to help our parents get up to snuff, but also to make sure that we do everything we can to have two-parent families. There's nothing like a mom and a dad to help kids be successful in school. These are the ideas that make a real difference in education.

We've got to raise the bar folks, or the future is not going to be as bright as the past.

Let me turn to another topic and that's capital. Of course capital flows quite easily around the world, but even so new ideas and new technologies tend to be funded by people who are close to home. My venture capital experience taught me that companies close to where we lived and where we work had a better chance to get funded than those that were far around the world. Capital at home today is quite plentiful, but ultimately capital here is enhanced when people are investing their savings in the economy—in the future.

> We've got to raise the bar folks, or the future is not going to be as bright as the past.

And that chart up there shows that our savings rate is looking pretty grim.

The bars that are upward in number show that two, three percent kind of savings rate that we've had over the past several years, but in the last year-and-a-half, we actually have a negative personal savings rate. Now the government has come up with all sorts of savings programs for our families. I'm told there are as many as 20 different plans. They present a daunting phalanx of penalties and rules. The government lets us save, but only if we do it in the way the nanny state tells us we can save.

It's time to make saving easy in America. I believe people should be allowed to earn interest dividends and capital gains, up to a certain amount per year, tax-free and without restrictions on how or when their savings or investments are spent. As an example, let's take the number of 5,000 bucks. Let's say, and that's not a final number, but let's use 5,000 dollars as an example for joint filers. What I'd say is people ought to be able to save annually or to be able to receive income annually, in capital gains, dividends in interest on

5,000 bucks and not have to pay any taxes on it at all, and not have to worry where that investment got spent. This would help the middle class to be able to invest and save. It also would allow them to spend their savings the way that Americans like to spend their savings—any way they want.

Let me turn to free trade for a moment. My growth factors—don't show the chart yet, we'll get there in a second. My growth factors include free trade. There'll be a growing clamor in this country for isolation and protectionism. Just wait for that '08 campaign to get under way, you're going to hear it time and time again. Protectionism might feel good for a few years, but then we'd be passed by the products that met the new world competitive standards like we were standing still. Protectionism would virtually guarantee that America would become a second-tier economy in a couple of decades, with a second-class standard of living.

At the same time we have to make sure that the rules of free trade are fair. It's time to make sure China's markets, for instance, are open to our goods. And it's time to ensure they enforce our intellectual property rights as well as they enforce their own. Try to counterfeit an Olympic tee-shirt in Beijing, for instance, and see how long it takes for them to find you. No, the easy money for the criminal counterfeiters is in software, entertainment, pharmaceuticals: the things that we export.

Fair trade has to be fair in both directions, but don't forget, it's good for all of us.

Let's look at technology. Without serious question, America is the innovation capital of the world.

That chart you can put up now shows the patents issued by the U.S. Patent Office. The red bars are patents issued to American enterprises, the yellow are those that come from all the other nations in the world. We lead the world, one country leads the entire world in patent applications.

The Internet started here, biotech is headquartered here, Microsoft is here. But China and other nations aren't going to just cede permanently our leadership in innovation and technology.

Now and then I hear people say that it's probably good economics for manufacturing to go from here; to go to Asia, because they can do it there cheaper. Then they go on and say, "But we'll continue to keep the design and engineering right here, they'll just do the manufacturing." But that belies very little experience in the real world. My experience is that design and innovation ultimately are done best next to manufacturing. Those that are proximate tend to get the best designs and the most innovative ideas. If the Chinese are making a product, you better expect them someday to be engineering it and designing it as well. It's critical, therefore, that America maintain our lead in manufacturing, if we also want to maintain our lead in innovation.

Now you know that where America invests in technology we lead the world. Places like healthcare and defense technology. Let me just show you a chart that shows how our investment dollars are spent at the federal government level.

The dark blue portion of that bar is money spent in health and the other areas are in the lines below. I'd like to make sure that we review how government invests our research dollars, because I want to see more research dollars going into power generation, fuel technology, materials science. I think it's critical that America continue to invest in our future in technology. It is what will allow us to lead the nations of the world for generations to come.

Now I mentioned five of the factors which accelerate our growth. How about those that slow down our growth? Let me look at those. Here's where they've seen, perhaps, the most dramatic change over the last 30 years.

I was with BiBi Netanyahu, the prime minister of Israel. He said that when he came into Israel that the economy was shrinking, not growing. He said as he looked at what was going on and talked to business leaders, he said it reminded him a bit of the first day of basic training in the Israeli army. They lined everybody up along a football field, they said take the person next to you and put them on your shoulders, we're going to have a race. And he said he had a big guy on his shoulders, so he couldn't run very fast. But somebody next to him had a real small guy on his shoulders and he won the race. He said the guy running the race, those are your corporations, your enterprises, your inventors. The guy on the shoulders, that's your government. And if government's too big it slows down the inventors and the entrepreneurs.

Now BiBi didn't come up with this all by himself. Ronald Reagan saw the same thing back in 1982. He and his team initiated a three-part strategy for our sclerotic economy. He said number one, we need to have a steady monetary policy, number two, deregulate, number three, we want sweeping tax cuts. Those three ingredients, low inflation, deregulation and tax relief, lay the foundation for an economic renaissance, and help to unleash the spirit of enterprise in this country. What Alex de Tocqueville had once called America's restlessness of temper. By contrast the European path led to high unemployment and anemic job growth.

Now the big issue we're going to face coming soon is taxes. What is the better course for America? A European model of high taxes and regulations, or low taxes and free trade, the Ronald Reagan model? That's the choice the next president is going to make. Some of course are already working hard to implement a massive tax increase.

Let me show you what it would look like. On the left-hand portion of that chart where you see the squiggly line go up and down, that's the taxation in the United States, the federal taxation is a percentage of GDP. It's gone up and down but pretty much level, over a bunch of years, around 18 percent. You'll see that big decline in the middle of the graph, that's what happened when President Bush instituted the tax cuts, as well as the recession in our economy. When the economy went south he said we need to lower taxes to get it going again and boy did it work, seven-million new jobs later. The chart to the right shows what would happen, the top line, if you saw a big tax cut, tax increase rather. That shows what would happen if the Bush tax cuts were allowed to expire. You'd see a massive tax increase, which without question would halt this economy in its tracks. If you see the flat line around 18 percent, that's what happens if the Bush tax cuts are made permanent. So its pretty simple, isn't it? It's absolutely critical that we don't have that massive tax hike and instead we make the Bush tax cuts permanent.

We need reform of our tax code. We need to move it toward a system that's encouraging of growth, fairness and simplicity. Now of course some people want to increase taxes because they want to spend more. When the party that's been in charge has been our own, I'm a little embarrassed to say that we haven't distinguished ourselves by reining in spending. The chart that I'm going to show now, go ahead, shows spending by year in non-military discretionary accounts.

The last few years there aren't as low as I'd like them to be. If we're serious about holding down taxes, we have to be serious about fundamental reforms to government and to entitlements. I have a pretty simple idea about how to keep our spending in check: give Congress a specific spending number and insist that that number is hit. If Congress doesn't hit that target, then its appropriations bills shall be vetoed. I regularly exercised my veto power when I was governor.

The alternative of course is for the Congress to vest the President with a power held by governors in some 43 states, including my state, the line-item veto.

And it's time, at long last, that the federal government is taken through the kind of cost and quality improvement process, and the kind of benchmarking process, and the kind of best practices process, that you in the private enterprise world carry on almost every single year. The duplication and waste, and inefficiency in government is absolutely mind boggling.

Our greatest challenge though is in entitlements. This next chart shows entitlements as a percentage of GDP.

The bar on the left is where we are right now. A little over 8 percent of GDP is spent on Medicare, Medicaid and Social Security. Fifty years from now the bar on the right would be in existence. That would say that we would be spending about 18 to 20 percent of our entire GDP on those entitlements. If you recall from my earlier slide, that is the total amount of taxation we receive. That would say that on the current trend, these entitlements would completely take over the federal budget and taxes would have to go through the roof. Our economy would be stalled.

Today's seniors are living in a world that almost no one could have imagined. The inventiveness and vitality of our pharmaceutical and biotech industries and our healthcare providers have meant ground-breaking advances and long life and I say it is worth it.

But when Social Security and Medicare were created, they were meant to solve a particular need—seniors living in poverty and without healthcare. They have done that. Now it's time to address a new set of challenges.

In the case of Social Security—we know the levers we can pull to bring it under control. It is time for Republicans and Democrats to come together and agree on a solution. Medicare and Medicaid are going to require more fundamental reform to tame their runaway costs.

How to do it? Well some people are going to say the best way to reform health care is have the government take it over, a single payer system, let the tax payer pick up the bill. As P.J O'Rourke once said, "If you think health care is expensive now, wait till it is free."

My suggestion is that the European model for solving health care is not the model at all. There is an American reform model: apply free market principles and individual responsibility. We took steps to do that in my state this last year. Here are the keys.

Make sure that the consumer of health services cares how much those services cost. Number two, get everyone in the system. You can't have people showing up at the hospital expecting free care because that ends up being passed on to everybody else.

Let me turn to another topic, tort reform. It's a big burden on our economic future. Last year, I was shocked to see that U.S. corporations spent more money defending tort claims than they spent on research and development.

I spoke with one member of the plaintiff's bar the other day. He said that tort lawyers are O.K. with state level tort reform, just not federal tort reform. You know what that means—as long as there is one lawsuit-friendly state, they can sue virtually any deep-pockets company in America. No thanks, America needs national tort reform.

Our regulatory burden is overbearing. I'd re-institute a regulatory relief board to cut back on the regulations that choke off growth.

Energy. Another burden on our future is our dependence on foreign energy. Every year, we spend hundreds of billions of dollars, sending it to countries for oil imports, and many of those countries don't like us. It's bad for our economy, it's bad for our foreign policy, it's bad for our environment. A reasonable and thoughtful energy equation has to have two sides.

On one side is supply—it means developing alternative sources of energy, liquefied coal, nuclear power, biofuels, and other sources of renewable energy. It also means investing to develop new technology, and obtaining oil from domestic sources such as oil shale, enhanced oil recovery, ANWR and the Outer Continental Shelf.

The other side of the equation is demand. We need to become more energy efficient—we use twice as much energy per person as a European, four times as much energy as the Japanese. Pursuing policies to reduce our per capita energy consumption is a critical step towards becoming energy independent.

This kind of a national goal of energy independence can't be achieved by simply counting on the market to do its job. And that is because the oil market is managed by a cartel. It makes no sense to continue to live in a fiction that says it behaves like a market. We cannot allow our future and our growth and prosperity to be held in the grip of an oil cartel, particularly when it includes people like Chavez and Ahmadinejad. What does this mean for Detroit? Well, it means that the automotive fleet will have to become more fuel efficient. CAFÉ improved mileage initially, but the consumer has gotten around it over the last couple of decades. You've seen the chart.

This next chart shows fuel economy rising like crazy from 75 to 80 as those CAFÉ requirements came into place. And then it has actually been flat to downward ever since.

> Let's not forget though that a far more efficient fuel fleet is going to be necessary for our energy future.

CAFÉ has some real problems as a vehicle for bringing down average fleet economy. It distorts the market. It penalizes the domestic automakers. It can ignore technical realities. So before I'd change the CAFÉ standards, I want to sit down with every major knowledgeable party and evaluate the alternatives. A good number have been proposed; let's decide which is the best course by looking at the data and carrying out analysis, rather than by playing to the TV cameras.

Let's not forget though that a far more efficient fuel fleet is going to be necessary for our energy future. The issue is to find the least distorting way to accomplish that goal.

By the way, I get a little tired of listening to supposed experts coming on TV and saying that Detroit just can't make cars that Americans want. Domestic cars, as you know, are burdened with over $2,000 more in healthcare and pension costs than a car that comes from Toyota for instance. To be competitive, American innovators right here in Michigan have come up with what I will call, wow styling—look at the Dodge for instance; super quality—look at the Ford Fusion; and extraordinary power plant fuel economies—look at the Chevy Silverado. As the son of an old auto guy, I got to say, I think Detroit deserves to be proud!

America faces new challenges. Some are unprecedented. If we fail to react, to adjust, we could fall behind our potential. The standard of living of our citizens could fail to keep pace. The future could be less prosperous than the past.

There are some who insist that the way to address these new challenges is by growing government, growing spending, raising taxes, protecting ourselves from the rest of the world by building isolating barriers and regulations. A government-centered strategy has been tried before, first by the Soviets, then by European welfare states. It has led to economic stagnation, falling standards of living and high unemployment. To take the same path they have taken and expect a different destination is foolishness.

It is the American way that leads to a brighter future for our children, to higher incomes, to a more secure employment, and to a more secure retirement. The American way, tested and proven, is low taxes, open markets, low burdens on employment, excellent education, good healthcare and reliable energy.

The American way will help us build a new American dream, for all Americans. It will be built in strong families and good schools, by innovative and nimble businesses, and by leaders who know that it is the people of America—free, hard-working, innovative people— that make America the hope of the world. Thank you so much.

Smarter Trade that Puts Workers First

John Edwards

Candidate for 2008 Democratic presidential nomination, 2006– ; born Seneca, NC, June 10, 1953; B.S., textile management, North Carolina State University, 1974; J.D., University of North Carolina School of Law, 1977; associate, Dearborn & Ewing, 1978; attorney, Tharrington, Smith & Hargrove, 1981–93; partner, Edwards & Kirby, 1993–98; U.S. senator (D), North Carolina, 1999–2005; candidate for 2004 Democratic presidential nomination; 2004 Democratic vice presidential nominee; director, Center on Poverty, Work, and Opportunity, University of North Carlina School of Law, 2005–06.

Editor's introduction: Edwards delivered the following speech in Cedar Rapids, IA, as part of a lecture series titled "American Political Leaders on the Future of U.S. Relations with Asia." Cosponsored by the National Committee on U.S.–China Relations, the series also featured Sam Brownback, a Republican senator from Kansas, and the Democratic Governors Bill Richardson, of New Mexico, and Tom Vilsack, of Iowa. In his speech, Edwards reflects on how globalization has impacted American jobs.

John Edwards's speech: Good morning. It's good to be back in Iowa with all of you today. I was recently here to talk about the fundamental unfairness at the heart of our economy today and what we need to do to fix it. I focused then on our tax code and how we can reform it to honor work, not just wealth. And in the coming weeks I will address the issue of corporate responsibility.

Today, I want to talk to you about one of the most important economic issues facing America—trade, especially its effect on jobs.

Over the past few years, I've traveled across this country and met with so many honest, hard working Americans, including many right here in Iowa, who've been left behind by our economy.

During one of my trips a couple of years ago, I met Doug Bishop. For years, Doug worked at the Maytag plant in Newton. He worked hard for Maytag day in and day out. And then Maytag decided to cut costs by cutting Doug's job.

Doug was lucky. After eight months out of work, he's back on his feet now, a leader in his community. But many other people in Newton—and across America—haven't been so lucky. They're as eager to get back to work as Doug was, but they're still struggling.

Delivered on August 6, 2007, at Cedar, Rapids, IA. Reprinted with permission.

These people did everything our country asked of them. Everything. They had jobs, they worked hard at them, and they provided for their families—and in return, they got the rug pulled out from under them. Who was looking out for these workers in Newton? Who was looking out for their families?

Not Maytag. And certainly not anyone in Washington, D.C.

It hasn't always been this way. Workers for generations were at the heart of our country. Hard-working men and women have made America the strongest, most prosperous nation in the history of the world. But today, Washington has turned its back on our workers and their futures.

More than ever, workers face an uncertain world where they feel like no one in Washington is doing what they can to help them.

They're right. Washington isn't looking out for them. Washington is too busy looking out for big business and protecting irresponsible corporations.

Trade has become a bad word for working Americans for a simple reason—*our trade policies have been bad for working Americans.* Washington looks at every trade deal and asks one question, and only one question—is it good for corporate profits?

They don't look at what it will do to workers, to families, to wages, to jobs, or even to the economy. When it comes to trade, the only thing that matters in Washington is the big business bottom line.

And most of big business is only looking out for its profits, not its people. Instead, they should be paying attention to a simple truth—corporations can be successful and responsible at the same time.

We need new trade policies in America that put workers, wages and families first. Not fourth, not third, not second. First. What we need is trade without trade-offs. Trade without trade-offs for workers. Trade without trade-offs for jobs. Trade without trade-offs for the environment.

We need trade without trade-offs for *America.*

Corporations, and the executives who lead them, need to realize that creating American jobs is not only the responsible thing to do, it's the patriotic thing to do.

But that's certainly not what is happening today. America is bleeding jobs.

Since President Bush took office, 5 million jobs have been lost to trade, including many here in Iowa, and 15 million *more* jobs may move offshore within the next decade. And don't let anyone tell you it's just low-skilled jobs that we'll lose—it's also many of our country's high quality service and technology jobs—jobs that require advanced education such as in computer programming, radiology, call centers, and financial analysis.

But it doesn't begin or end with just the jobs being outsourced to China, India and elsewhere. The negative effects from globalization are ripping through the economy.

Globalization has helped stunt the growth in wages for American workers. Workers in America must now compete every day with workers overseas earning miserably low wages with no benefits. And what's even worse, big multinational corporations now use the excuse that they have to ship ever more good-paying American jobs overseas in order to compete with the very low wage jobs they themselves created there. In the last few years, wages have fallen for nearly every educational group, all the way up to masters degrees—and corporate profits have nearly doubled.

Rather than create income gains for all, the gains from globalization are mostly flowing to the most fortunate Americans. Globalization is a major reason why income inequality is at its worst since before the Great Depression.

It shouldn't be this way. And when I'm president, I'm going to tell the lobbyists pulling the strings in Washington and the big corporations that hire them the same thing—their time is over. The system is rigged against regular Americans to guarantee more power for the powerful and more wealth for the wealthy. Well, I'm going to cut the rigging down and end the game.

> Washington's values are all wrong, but the American people's values are exactly right. We believe in hard work, fairness and opportunity.

Washington's values are all wrong, but the American people's values are exactly right. We believe in hard work, fairness and opportunity. Just like we always have. And we're going to restore those values to our economy and our government.

I know the American people want change, real change. Washington isn't working for them. Our economy isn't working for them. But by uniting together, we can fix this. We can make sure that working and middle class families again have the opportunities to which they're entitled.

While CEOs have been sitting in their boardrooms and while lobbyists and Washington insiders having been dining in their steakhouses, I have been on the ground. Meeting workers. Walking picket lines. I've walked past far too many manufacturing plants with locks on their gates and weeds in their yards. I've heard firsthand from workers how they're one crisis away—one pink slip, one trip to the emergency room—from going over a cliff. But I've also seen firsthand their determination to fight—for their families and for our values.

We'll need courage and conviction and backbone to go up against these powerful lobbyists and insiders. Half measures and baby steps won't level the playing field. Triangulation and compromise won't fix anything. It won't be easy, but together—you and me and everyone who is sick of listening to Washington say one thing and do another—we can stand up and change this country for the better.

And we certainly need change, especially in our trade policies. For years now, Washington has been passing trade deal after trade deal that works great for multinational corporations, but not for working Americans.

For example, NAFTA and the WTO provide unique rights for foreign companies whose profits are allegedly hurt by environmental and health regulations. These foreign companies have used them to demand compensation for laws against toxins, mad cow disease, and gambling—they have even sued the Canadian postal service for being a monopoly. Domestic companies would get laughed out of court if they tried this, but foreign investors can assert these special rights in secretive panels that operate outside our system of laws.

When economists say that trade helps our economy overall, we need to be honest about the fact that it does not help everyone. The true measure of our economy isn't found only in the size of our GDP or the level of corporate profits—it's whether middle class families are doing better or worse.

A sure sign that our trade and economic policies are seriously out of whack is our trade deficit. Our nation's imports have increased by a staggering 50 percent in the past 15 years, and instead of a trade balance, the United States now has the largest trade deficit in the history of the globe—and it just keeps growing. Last year, our current account deficit was more than $850 billion, which is a staggering 6.5 percent of our nation's entire GDP, and our trade deficit with China alone was $233 billion. That means that we are consuming billions of dollars more in imported goods than we produce—and we are borrowing heavily to pay for them.

Behind all these numbers and statistics are the faces of millions of Americans forgotten in our trade deals. Well, I can tell you that I will never forget them. I saw what happened when the mill that my dad worked in all his life, and that I worked in myself when I was young, closed and the jobs went somewhere else. It wasn't just devastating to our community economically—it was devastating to the pride and dignity of the people who worked hard every day trying to make a better life for their kids.

Let me tell you, if a CEO thinks the right thing to do is to ship American jobs overseas, to destroy families and communities, then I challenge him to go and look those workers in the eye and have the guts to tell them to their face that they can't compete. I've stood with these workers all across America—and let me tell you, they can compete, because they are the best workers in the world.

The trade policies of President Bush have devastated towns and communities all across America. But let's be clear about something—this isn't just his doing. For far too long, presidents from both parties have entered into trade agreements, agreements like NAFTA, promising that they would create millions of new jobs and enrich communities. Instead, too many of these agreements have cost us jobs and devastated many of our towns.

NAFTA was written by insiders in all three countries, and it served their interests—not the interests of regular workers. It included unprecedented rights for corporate investors, but no labor or environmental protections in its core text. And over the past 15 years, we have seen growing income inequality in the U.S., Mexico and Canada.

Well enough is enough. Americans have paid the price long enough. We need to change our fundamental approach to trade. We need to make American values the foundation of our trade deals, and we need to put workers back at their core.

Let me tell you, no one is asking for any guarantees. America has the most open economy in the world, and no one is suggesting that we put up tariffs or go back to protectionism. Any politician who promises to bring back the jobs we've lost isn't telling the truth—no one can bring back those jobs. But with a level playing field, American workers can compete with anybody on earth. And I'm absolutely not suggesting an end to trade.

I am calling instead for an end to lip service. Our leaders in Washington say many of the right things. They even say that they will make sure the gains from trade are shared with everyone. But when push comes to shove, the trade gets pushed forward and the sharing gets shoved off.

We can and we must change this. I believe we need to follow three principles to make sure globalization works for everyone.

First, trade deals must benefit workers, not just big multinational corporations. Today, our trade agreements are negotiated behind closed doors. The multinationals get their say, but when one goes to Congress it gets an up or down vote—no amendments are allowed. No wonder that corporations get unique protections, while workers don't benefit. That's wrong.

Imagine trade policies that actually put American workers first. We need fair rules for workers, and we need strong protections for labor and the environment and against currency manipulation. If a deal is good for middle class families, it's good for America; if it's not, it's not.

Second, our trade policies should also lift up workers around the world. This struggle over fair trade is about more than just what's at stake for America's workers—it's also about what's at stake for workers in every country. Making sure that workers around the globe are treated fairly and share in trade gains is the right thing to do morally, it's the right thing to do economically, and it will make us much safer and more secure. That's what strong labor standards are all about. Making sure that workers have the right to organize and earn a fair wage will not only prevent a "race to the bottom" on labor rights—it will also help build a global middle class that shares in the gains from trade and creates markets for U.S. exports.

Third, we need to address more than just our trade policies in order to restore fairness and opportunity to workers. I talked earlier about some of the adverse effects of globalization—stagnant wages and rising inequality. To help regular Americans get ahead and stay ahead, we need to make sure our children get a quality education and have the chance to go to college. We need to raise the minimum wage, strengthen unions, and help families build assets. And the most important thing we can do to provide security to our workers is to guarantee universal health care in this country. I am proud to be the first major candidate to come out with a plan for universal health care.

We also need to invest resources to ensure that our country keeps its competitive edge in the world. We need to create the jobs of the future right here in America and make sure our workers have the skills they need to fill them. We need to make the Research and Experimentation Tax Credit permanent, invest in life sciences and biomedical research, strengthen math and science education, and create a new energy economy.

There are so many things we can do to put our economy back on the side of the working men and women who make this country great. Our trade policies have a huge impact on whether regular Americans—in Iowa and across the country—have the chance to get ahead in our economy or whether they are left behind.

> It is not enough for a trade deal to be popular on Wall Street or show up in economic statistics.

We need a new era in trade policy. We need "smart trade" policies that American workers can say yes to— trade policies that do more than pay lip service to their needs and that actually make sure prosperity is shared. Trade policies that are as innovative as the American people. And when I'm president, those are the trade policies we will have.

And let me be clear: we will make sure that these policies are in place before we pass a single new trade deal.

In my first year in office, I will spend time working with Congress to get our trade policies straight—policies which ensure that Americans workers finally begin to see benefits from the global economy. And then, when we negotiate new trade deals it won't just be big multinational corporations whose interests are served—it will also be the interests of American workers, America's communities, and our global environment.

First, I will be a tough negotiator on new trade deals. There are good trade deals and there are bad trade deals, and when I am president it will be crystal clear that we have a president who knows the difference. It is not enough for a trade deal to be popular on Wall Street or show up in economic statistics. My main measure is just this one—after considering the impact on jobs, wages and prices, will most families be better off? When I'm president, our trade agreements will give workers fair and level playing fields. All our trade partners must meet basic labor standards, such as prohibiting sweatshops and child labor and protecting the right of workers to join unions. These conditions should be the floor, not the ceiling. And they should not be in side agreements, but at the core of the agreements. I will tie unilateral trade preferences and bilateral trade agreements to progress on labor rights. As president, I will also push the World Trade Organization to begin to address labor standards. And I will build on the precedent of the Cambodia textiles agreement, which rewarded progress on labor rights with greater market access. New trade agreements must also include strong rules on environmental protection and against currency manipulation. As the world's biggest customer, our trade deals can be vital tools to ensure that progress is made in stopping global warming. They can also be tools to ensure that poor environmental practices do not create unfair competitive advantages. Second, I will insist that our trade deals be fairly and fully administered. For free trade to be fair, it must be based on rules, and then those rules must be followed. But right now, many major U.S. trading partners are breaking the rules without any consequences.

As president, I will seek to restore America's moral leadership of the world, and our trade policies with these countries can help. But we are going to be tough in our negotiations because the overriding obligation of the president of the United States is to put America's workers, economy and national interests first.

Right now, China, India and certain other nations are each, to one degree or another, combining miserably low wages and poor environmental practices with tax breaks, subsidies, tariffs, low-cost loans, and currency manipulation to advance their trade at the expense of ours. All of this is costing Americans high-quality jobs and threatening millions more.

When I am president, restoring fair and balanced trade with China will be a particular priority. Its massive manipulation of the yuan has continued for years, giving it an unfair advantage against U.S. manufacturers, and its labor and intellectual property protections are grossly inadequate. As a result of the massive trade deficits we run with China—the largest ever between any two countries, more than $230 billion last year alone—China now owns $1 trillion in U.S. assets, giving it great leverage over our economy and our security. This is not acceptable. We need to persuade China's authoritarian government to commit to the rules that govern the conduct of responsible nations. Our trade policies are a great opportunity for increased leverage over China. And, when I'm president I will make it crystal clear that doing business with China should not come at the expense of American jobs or our economy— there must and will be balance between our nations when we trade.

As for our good friend India, which has achieved remarkable economic growth in recent years, we still must work hard to get it to adhere to both the letter and the spirit of its trade agreements with the U.S. and to further achieve our shared values, while all the while improving the lives of its millions of citizens.

I know following the letter of any law, let alone trade law, isn't a priority for the Bush administration, but it will be for mine. In the Edwards administration, the top prosecutors at the Department of

Justice will be responsible for enforcing our trade agreements. Right now, the trade negotiators charged with enforcing agreements seem to think their job is done when an agreement is signed. Signing a trade deal should be the beginning of the process, not the end. And I will insist that we finally begin to prosecute illegal foreign subsidies, currency manipulation, and trade practices.

Fair terms of trade also mean fixing our own tax code so that corporations aren't rewarded for closing plants and shipping jobs to countries like China. Our government should be encouraging businesses to invest here. Yet, one of the starkest examples that our economy works best for big business instead of regular Americans is that we actually give tax incentives to companies to invest overseas. American companies setting up shop in tax havens often pay little or no U.S. tax. This is not only wrong, it's unpatriotic. I will eliminate the tax incentives that encourage companies to invest overseas rather than here at home. These dollars, if invested in new facilities and in retraining workers and rebuilding devastated communities, can fuel a dramatic expansion of our own economy. Third, we need much more investment in helping the workers and communities left behind. When we sign a trade deal, we know which industries and workers will likely be affected by greater competition. We need to restore some honesty to the trade debate and not claim, like too many presidents from both parties have done, that trade will help everyone. This is simply not true.

When I am president, every trade agreement will be subject to not only an economic assessment showing how imports and exports will be affected by the agreement, but also to a "community impact assessment." We need to make sure trade deals produce real benefits that are widely shared, and we need to get a head start on helping any workers and communities who will be hurt by increases in imports or by competition from other countries. Before I ask Congress to approve any new trade agreement, we will have an honest discussion about the real impact of that agreement on towns and communities and workers across our country.

Then we can go into dislocated communities—starting before the jobs are gone—and help them diversify their economies with initiatives modeled on the military base closing commissions, bringing local leaders, employers and unions together to rebuild local economies. We need to be much more aggressive about helping workers and affected communities.

Training is no substitute for good trade policies, but we must help workers gain new skills and get ahead. The problem is that, too often, training programs are completely disconnected from the job market. I will create a broad new Training Works program that ties retraining to real jobs. It will support on-the-job training programs through partnerships among businesses, unions and community colleges. Workers will be trained on-the-job to make sure the jobs actually exist. And to make it worth businesses' while—and to support high-wage jobs—we will pay part of workers' wages while they are being trained.

All types of workers are affected by globalization, and all types of workers should be eligible for help getting back on their feet. But Trade Adjustment Assistance, or TAA, now only helps manufacturing workers at plant closings.

Because most unemployed workers who lose their jobs aren't even covered by unemployment insurance, I will help states modernize their programs. This will give security to 500,000 more jobless workers a year, including more low-wage and part-time workers.

And, as we have seen over the last year, another dark side of trade is the concern over the safety of the foods we eat, the toys our children play with, and even the medicines we take.

Now more than ever, we need to make sure that our trade rules protect American consumers.

Food imports have doubled in the past decade, and Americans now eat three-quarters of a pound of imported food every day. However, less than 1 percent of imported food is inspected.

As president, I will enforce mandatory "country of origin" labeling for food and other consumer products so that Americans will know who is making the products they are buying. The big meat packers have blocked this law for too long. I will give the FDA all the authority and resources it needs to keep tainted food and products out of our country and out of our homes.

We will strengthen enforcement to ensure that safety standards are being met, and we will enforce "zero tolerance" and immediately freeze the specific import of any food, toys, medicines, or other goods that threatens the health of our children and families. We will not let them in until we know they are safe, because the health and welfare of our children are more important than cheap toys.

We must make sure that trade is not only smart and good for America's economy and workers, but safe for American families. Regular families—their safety and their best interests—should come before the interests of multinational corporations. That's what safe and smart trade is about.

You know, some people as they listen to my new smart trade vision for America will accuse me of being a protectionist or anti-trade. They would be wrong. I believe in smart and safe trade, just not trade that helps American multinationals but hurts America.

And, let me tell you, you can protect the interests of American workers and still trade. We can grow our economy, and create good jobs and trade responsibly, fairly and safely. With smart trade policies, we can make sure American workers compete on level playing fields. With smart trade policies, we can create a new future where even more workers and their families have a chance to achieve the American Dream.

I know we can make trade and our economy work for regular workers, but real change must first begin with ending—once and for all—the influence lobbyists have on trade policies and on our government. It's time Washington worked for the American people, not for lobbyists and insiders. It's time that the president stood up and fought for American workers. It's time to have a president that always—always—puts the interests of the American people first.

So today, I'm again calling on all federal officeholders and candidates from all political parties to join me in putting an end to the money game in Washington by simply refusing to accept any form of campaign donation from federal lobbyists going forward. It's really just that simple. We need to send a message to all of the lobbyists in Washington: Your money is no good here, and we're not going to take it anymore. We don't need you, we've got the American people on our side.

What I've just said today isn't going to be popular with the special interest groups, lobbyists or Washington insiders. But this isn't about being well-liked. This is about doing what's right.

They're going to try to distract you and me from the issues that matter—issues like health care, poverty, jobs and economic fairness.

And it's these insiders in Washington who are going to attack us to try to keep people like me from speaking out, but they won't succeed. Because I'm going to fight with every breath I have. Because this isn't about me or them—it's about you, your family, your children, and how those who run for president are going to fight for real change to create a better America where all of us can go as far as our hard work and God-given talents will take us.

That's the kind of president I will be.

As Harry Truman said, "The ultimate test of any presidential decision is 'not whether it's popular at the time, but whether it's right . . . If it's right, make it, and let the popular part take care of itself.'"

We know we don't have to live in an America where hard-working men and women are struggling to get by. Where we pass trade deal after trade deal that rip apart communities. Where good people like those who worked at Maytag do right by their country and are still left out in the cold.

That's not our America. Our America says if you work hard, you'll have the chance to get ahead and leave your kids a better life. That's the One America we're fighting for. That's our America. And together, I know we can make our One America a reality because the real power of America isn't in Washington, it's with the American people. It's with all of you.

And that is why when I'm president, real change is coming.

Thank you. God bless you. God bless America.

III. HEALTH CARE REFORM

Speech to the American Hospital Association (AHA) Annual Membership Meeting

George W. Bush

President of the United States, 2001– ; born New Haven, CT, July 6, 1946, and raised in Midland and Houston, TX; attended Phillips Academy, Andover, MA; B.A., Yale University, 1968; M.B.A., Harvard Business School, 1975; F-102 pilot, Texas Air National Guard, 1968–73; oil and gas business, Midland, TX, 1975–86; senior adviser in father George H. W. Bush's presidential campaign, 1987–88; one of the partners who purchased the Texas Rangers baseball franchise, 1989, and managing general partner of the team, 1989–94; governor of Texas, 1995–2000.

Editor's introduction: Health care reform remains a pivotal issue in the 2008 presidential campaign. While the Democratic candidates have proposed various initiatives to control costs and extend health care coverage to more—if not all—Americans, the Bush administration has offered its own solutions, which rely on free-market based reforms rather than government intervention. As Bush states in the following speech, which he delivered at the Washington Hilton Hotel, "The best way to reform this health care system is to preserve the system of private medicine." Among the president's proposed initiatives are five central features: expanded health savings accounts (HSAs); greater transparency so that patients understand more about procedures and their costs; modern information technology, including electronic medical records; increased discounts for small businesses; and tort reform.

George W. Bush's speech: Thank you very much. It was on this stage two nights ago that I had the pleasure of showing up with a George W. Bush look-alike. So I walked in and Dick said, is it really you?

Thanks for your introduction, Dick. Thanks for the invitation to be here. I want to, first, thank all the good people of the American Hospital Association. I appreciate the important voice that you provided for our hospitals, but more importantly, I appreciate the compassionate care you give to our citizens.

I have come to talk about a comprehensive health care strategy that will make health care more affordable and available for all our citizens. And I appreciate you giving me a chance to use this forum as an opportunity to discuss our vision for moving forward.

Delivered on May 1, 2006, at Washington, D.C.

I do want to thank George Lynn, who is the Chairman of the American Hospital Association Board of Trustees. I want to thank all the trustees who are here. I appreciate the leadership of the American Hospital Association. I want to thank the members of the American Hospital Association.

I understand—there he is—my friend, Charlie Norwood is here. Good to see you, Congressman. Thank you so much for being here. You're looking pretty good. Looking real good, as a matter of fact.

This economy of ours is strong, and that's important for health care. It's important for the hospitals. And the economy is getting stronger. We put our trust in the American people by cutting taxes, and the tax relief we passed is saving—is helping people save and spend and invest. And when people save, spend and invest, it causes our economy to grow. Thanks to tax relief and pro-growth economic policies, we're now in our fifth year of uninterrupted economic growth.

In the first quarter of this year, the economy grew at 4.8 percent. We've had 18 straight quarters of economic expansion. Last year our economy grew faster than any other major industrialized nation. Over the past two-and-a-half years, we've created 5.1 million new jobs, and that's more than Japan and the 25 nations of the EU combined. Productivity is high; the unemployment rate is 4.7 percent; consumer confidence is at its highest point ever—in nearly four years. The new economic report out today contains good news on income growth.

Things are looking good for this economy. But we cannot be complacent. One of my concerns is that the United States of America loses our nerve, fears competition and we become an isolated and protectionist nation. And health care plays a vital role in making sure this nation remains competitive.

One of the best ways to make sure that we're a competitive nation is to continue to invest in research and technology. If America wants to be the leader of the world, we've got to remain on the leading edge of change. As many of you know, when I came into office I pledged to continue the doubling of the funding for the National Institutes of Health, and we kept that commitment. And it's one of the many reasons why our health care system leads the world. And we need to keep—we need to understand the importance of research at the federal level, and that's why I have proposed that the United States Congress double federal investment in basic scientific research.

In other words, for this country to be competitive we've got to invest in the future. See, I don't think we ought to fear the future, I don't think we ought to become protectionists and isolationists. I think we need to continue to lead. And one way to lead is to lead in research and development.

To keep this economy competitive with other nations around the world, we've got to do something about our dependence on oil. Dependency on oil creates an economic problem for us, and it creates a national security problem for us. So I look forward to working with Congress to change—to help speed up research and development so we can change our habits, so we can drive cars fueled by ethanol, or so we can have batteries that enable cars to drive for the first 40 miles on electricity.

To keep this country competitive, we've got to have a health care system that provides our people with good quality care at affordable prices. In other words, you're a part of an industry that must be reformed in order for the United States to continue to be an economic leader.

America has the best health care system in the world, pure and simple. We got the best medicines, we got the best doctors, and we have the best hospitals. And we intend to keep it that way. Yet, we are challenged by the fact that health care costs are rising sharply. In the past five years, private health insurance premiums have risen 73 percent. And as a result, some businesses have been forced to drop health care coverage for their employees. You know that as well as anybody. Others have been forced to raise co-payments and premiums. Some have been paying increasing health care costs and, therefore, have been unable to give workers the pay raises they need to cope with rising health care costs.

We lead the world in health care because we believe in a system of private medicine that encourages innovation and change.

With rising costs, many Americans are concerned. They're concerned they're not going to be able to afford health care. As you well know, millions of our fellow citizens have no health insurance at all. And as you know, that places burdens on our nation's hospitals. This is unacceptable for this country to have health care costs rising as fast as they are. If we want to be the leader of the world, we must do something about it. And my administration is determined to do something about it.

To make our health care system work for all Americans, we have to choose between two philosophies: one that trusts government to make the best decisions for the people's health care, or one that trusts the people and their doctor to make the best decisions for their health care.

We know from experience which of these systems works best. Other nations that have opted for bigger government and more centralized control now have long waits for treatment for the people. The quality of care is lower. There's less technological innovation. In America, as you know, we follow a different path. We lead the world in health care because we believe in a system of private medicine that encourages innovation and change.

And the best way to reform this health care system is to preserve the system of private medicine, is to strengthen the relationship between doctors and patients, and make the benefits of private medicine more affordable and accessible for all our citizens.

Government has a role to play. Don't get me wrong. We're kind of—we're big in the health care field, as you may know. We have a major role to play in strengthening and reforming this health care system, but in a way that preserves the doctor-patient relationship.

And that's what I want to talk to you about today. The first goal of our health care strategy is to meet the obligation the federal government has made to take care of the elderly and the poor. We have said, as a federal government, we will help the elderly and the poor. And I intend to keep that obligation. We're meeting that obligation, that responsibility through Medicare, Medicaid, and community health centers.

More than four decades ago, the federal government established Medicare to provide health coverage for older Americans. The bill was signed by Lyndon Baines Johnson. He came from a state I know pretty well. When I came into office I found a Medicare program that was outdated, a Medicare program that was not meeting the needs of America's seniors. The way I tried to explain it to the American people was this: We had a system that would pay $28,000 for an ulcer surgery, but not the $500 it would cost for prescription drugs that would prevent the ulcer from being—from taking hold in the first place. And that didn't make any sense—$28,000 for the surgery, but not a dime of prescription drugs to prevent the surgery from being needed. To me that's an outdated system. It's one that's not very cost-effective, and it's one that does not provide quality care for our seniors.

So I decided to do something about it. And I worked with the Congress, and we passed critical legislation that modernizes Medicare and provides seniors with more choices to the private sector, and has given our seniors better access to the prescription drugs they need.

The benefit allows seniors to choose from a number of private prescription drug plans to find the one that is right for them. It encourages plan providers to compete for the seniors' business. And that helps lower costs. The new Medicare prescription drug benefit is a good deal for America's seniors. The typical senior will end up spending about half of what he or she used to spend on prescription drugs each year.

In addition, we've provided extra help for low-income seniors. About a third of the seniors are eligible for prescription drug coverage that includes low or no premiums, low deductibles, and no gaps in coverage. On average, Medicare will pay for more than 95 percent of the costs of prescription drugs for low-income seniors.

I know you shared my concern when we heard the stories of low-income seniors having to choose between food and medicine. And because of this reform, those days are over with.

The Medicare prescription drug benefit went into effect in January. More than 30 million people now have prescription drug coverage through the Medicare program, and hundreds of thousands more are signing up each week. We want every senior who needs coverage to sign up.

The May 15th deadline for seniors to sign up at the lowest cost is approaching. Over the next two weeks, this administration will encourage our nation's pharmacies—pharmacists and doctors and hospitals and others in the medical community to continue to get the word out to seniors about the benefits of this important program. There are some seniors who are risk-adverse, they don't want to change. It is really important for those of us who are involved in health care in this country to get the word out that, at the very minimum, seniors ought to look and see what's available. Americans need to take advantage of this opportunity to choose a plan.

We're also—I also recognize that we got a problem with the long-term viability of Medicare. Today, the trustees for our Medicare and Social Security systems will release their annual report. Each year the trustees remind us that these programs are not structured in a way that they will be financially sound for our children and our grandchildren.

The problem is pretty basic. There's a lot of baby boomers like me getting ready to retire. In my case, two-and-a-half years. And there's a lot of baby boomers who are living longer, and there are fewer workers per beneficiary paying money in the system to support future retirees like me. And so the systems are going broke. And now is the time to do something about it. We've got too much politics in Washington, D.C. It's time to set aside politics and restructure Social Security and Medicare for generations to come.

We're honoring our nation's commitments to take care of the poor by strengthening Medicaid. Medicaid is a program administered in conjunction with the states that provides health care for low-income families with children, poor seniors, and disabled Americans. To help improve Medicaid, earlier this year, I signed legislation to restructure Medicaid and give states more flexibility in designing better programs to cover their citizens.

Under the reforms I signed into law, it's now easier for states to offer alternative benefit plans, provide coverage to more people, and design their Medicaid program to meet their state's needs and budgets. In the coming months, my administration will be encouraging states to adopt common-sense reforms. Our health care system must be guided by the needs of patients, not by rules emanating out of Washington, D.C.

Another way we're meeting our commitment to Americans in need is through community health centers. These centers provide primary health care for the poor, so they don't have to go to the emergency room of a hospital to get routine care. This is a really good use of taxpayers' money. It makes a lot of sense to have community health centers so that we can cut down on unnecessary visits to the emergency rooms. Health centers help lower the cost of health care for everyone.

Since I took office we've funded about 800 new or expanded health centers, bringing our total to more than 3,700 health centers serving more than 13 million Americans a year. And over the next two years, we will fund the opening and expanding of 400 more health centers. And Congress needs to fully support these health centers in the budget that I have submitted.

And so we have got a strategy to take care—help our elderly and the poor and the disabled. But the second part of our strategy is to make care and coverage more affordable and available for Americans. And here are five key policies to support this goal.

Our first policy is to expand health savings accounts to help improve health care and to help lower costs. Under the current system, as you well know, most Americans have no idea what the actual cost of their treatment is. Third-party insurers pay their bills. So patients have no reason to demand better prices, and the health care industry is under little pressure to lower prices. When somebody else pays the bills, it seems like everything is just fine. The result is that health care costs are skyrocketing. The insurance companies pass these rising costs on to their workers, on to workers and their employees in the form of higher premiums.

Now, health savings accounts transform what I believe is an outdated system by putting patients in control of how their health care dollars are spent. And when patients and consumers see how their health care dollars are spent, they demand more value for their money. The result is better treatment at lower costs.

HSAs have two components: low-cost catastrophic insurance coverage, and tax-free savings accounts. The catastrophic coverage protects you and your family in the event of a devastating medical illness. The health savings account allows you or your employer to contribute to a tax-free account to pay for your routine medical needs. The money that goes into your account is tax-free, the interest earned on your account is tax-free, and the money withdrawn from your account is tax-free. It means that you own your money in your account, and that you can build your savings by rolling over contributions that you do not spend in any given year.

HSAs can help us move toward a health care system that is no longer dominated by third-party payers to a system in which consumers make their own decisions. And we see strong evidence that HSAs are making health care more affordable and accessible. From March 2005 to January 2006, the number of HSAs tripled from one million to more than three million. This is a new product. People are getting—taking a look at it. They're beginning to see the merits of a tax-free savings system coupled with catastrophic care.

Forty percent of the people who bought HSAs have family incomes below $50,000. HSAs are making health care more accessible for those without insurance. More than a third of those who bought

HSAs on their own had previously been uninsured. HSAs are good for small business owners. HSAs, in my judgment, will mean that Americans who do not have coverage will be able to get coverage and afford coverage, which is good for America's hospitals. You see, by making health care coverage more affordable, more Americans can afford insurance. And with more Americans insured, fewer people will show up at our nation's hospitals needing uncompensated care.

HSAs also create an incentive for patients to become more informed about their medical options and more involved in their treatment as they shop for the best value for their health dollar. This involvement strengthens the doctor-patient relationship.

Equally importantly is that HSA owners can see the benefits of changing risky behavior. They can follow doctors' preventative recommendations. The healthier you are, the less money you're going to spend out of your savings account. And there will be a tangible return—more of your own money tax-free. Some employers are even offering employees financial incentives to get regular check-ups and lose weight and get fit. By encouraging preventative medicine, HSAs save lives and save health care dollars.

HSAs will benefit hospitals, doctors, and patients, and they can also benefit hospital workers. Today, only a handful of hospitals offer HSAs to their employees. I encourage the members of the American Hospital Association to consider the benefits of offering health savings accounts to your employees. HSAs will provide your workers with better care and lower your health care costs.

For decades, America's hospitals and health care professionals have led the world in innovation and quality medical care. Now you have an opportunity to help America transform our health care system by choosing the innovation and quality of health savings accounts. As HSAs continue to grow in popularity, my administration is working to expand them to even more Americans.

One way to make HSAs more attractive is to make them portable so they can meet the practical needs of today's workers. Many people are changing jobs, and one of their greatest fears is that they will lose their health care coverage. We believe that no American should have to remain locked in a job to get health insurance. Today, the savings in your health account are portable, and that means you can take your savings accounts from job to job. However, the health insurance within your HSA account is often not portable, and this is because of outdated laws and practices that prevent insurers from offering portable policies. I believe health insurers should be able to sell portable HSA policies nationwide.

Another obstacle to expanding HSAs is the federal tax code. Under current law, employers and employees pay no income or payroll tax on any health insurance provided through the workplace. If you buy your own insurance, you do not get the same tax break. That means that the self-employed, or the unemployed, or workers at companies that do not provide health insurance are at a great disadvantage.

Congress needs to end this discrimination in the tax code and give Americans who buy HSA policies on their own the same tax breaks as those who get their health insurance from their employers.

The current tax code also limits the amount you contribute to your HSA tax-free. The limit is usually tied to your deductible. Sometimes your total out-of-pocket expenses are greater than your deductible. Those with chronic illnesses often have expenses that go well beyond their deductibles. So we need to fix the tax code by allowing Americans to cover their out-of-pocket expenses with tax-free dollars, and make HSAs even more practical for more American families.

In addition to these efforts to fix the code, I've proposed a refundable tax credit to help low-income Americans purchase health coverage on the individual market. Under my proposal low-income families can receive up to $3,000 in a refundable tax credit to purchase HSA-qualified insurance. By working together, we can reform our tax code and make it easier for American families to get health care.

> The second policy for making health care more affordable and accessible is to increase transparency in our health care system.

And this week, Congress takes an important step in these efforts. Congressman Eric Cantor of Virginia will introduce a bill that would end many of the biases in the tax code, provide a tax credit of up to $3,000 for low-income families, and make HSAs more attractive. It's a bill called the Tax-Free Health Savings Act.

I also want to thank Senators Burns and Allen, Ensign and DeMint for introducing bills to improve HSA options for all Americans, and Senators Santorum and Murkowski for introducing legislation supporting the low-income tax credit. Congress needs to pass these reforms, and make sure the doctor-patient relationship remains central to our health care system.

The second policy for making health care more affordable and accessible is to increase transparency in our health care system. To be smart consumers, we need to be informed consumers, and this is especially true for patients with HSAs who have an incentive to spend their HSA dollars wisely. They need to know in advance what their medical options are, the quality and expertise of the docs and the hospitals in the area in which they live, and what their medical procedures will cost.

My administration is working with the AHA and other health care associations to provide patients with reliable information about prices and quality on the most common medical procedures. And I want to thank the AHA board for adopting a resolution this week supporting transparency. I appreciate your leadership on this vital issue.

We must work together to get patients the information they need so they can get the best quality care for the best price. If you're worried about increasing costs, it makes sense to have price options available for patients. That's what happens in a lot of our society; it should happen in health care, as well. By increasing transparency, the idea is to empower consumers to find value for their dollars and to help patients find better care and to help transform this system of ours to make sure America remains the leader in health care.

Secretary Leavitt has met with leaders in the health care industry in 13 cities to encourage them to work with the Department of Health and Human Services to increase transparency in the marketplace. We're asking doctors and hospitals and other providers to post their walk-in prices to all patients.

I directed the Department of Health and Human Services to make data on Medicare's price and quality publicly available on the Internet. The first data will be available to all Americans by June 1st. We're also asking insurance companies to increase health care transparency by providing their negotiating prices and quality information to their enrollees. And the federal government will do the same.

My administration will be requiring transparency from insurance plans participating in federal programs. Beginning this year, the Federal Employees Benefit Program and the military's Tricare system are asking contractors to begin providing price and quality information.

Today, I'm asking for your help. Every hospital represented here should take action to make information on prices and quality available to all your patients. If everyone here cooperates in this endeavor we can increase transparency without the need for legislation from the United States Congress. By working together, transparency—to increase transparency, we can help lower costs.

The third policy is to provide modern information technology to our medical system. Too many doctors' offices and hospitals have the most advanced technology in the 21st century, but still use last century's filing systems. Doctors are still writing out files by hand. And that's kind of dangerous because most doctors don't write too well. In hospitals, there's more risk of medical error and duplicate tests when records are handwritten on paper instead of cross-checked on a computer.

So, in 2004, I set a goal that most Americans would have an electronic health record within 10 years. And we're making good progress toward that goal. The first thing is, we needed to develop a common standard of language so that health care providers in Los Angeles and health care providers in New York knew what the— knew what we are talking about.

Imagine how valuable this access to information will become. If you had someone who had an epileptic seizure outside their home town and ended up in a hospital in a nearby town, these electronic records would help save lives. Information would be valid and clear. There wouldn't be any confusion amongst those who are working hard to provide compassionate care.

As we develop an information network, nationwide information network, we will make sure that we protect the privacy of a patient's medical record. But make no mistake about it, bringing information technology into our health care system is going to reduce costs and increase quality care for American people.

And I hope you're aggressive on this front. I urge you to work with the AHA to come up with a plan to help develop a nationwide information system that is modern and helps you do your job better.

The fourth policy is to make it easier for small businesses to obtain the same discounts that big companies get when obtaining health care insurance. Unlike big businesses, small companies cannot negotiate lower health insurance rates because they can't spread their risk over a larger pool of employees. So we proposed association health plans that will allow small firms to band together across state lines and buy insurance at the same discounts available to big companies. The House has passed a bill. The Senate hasn't acted, and now it's time for the United States Senate to do something good for the small business employers of this country.

Our fifth policy to confront high cost health care and to make sure private medicine is central in the United States is to confront the glut of frivolous lawsuits that are driving good doctors out of practice and driving up the cost of health care.

To avoid junk lawsuits, professionals in the health care field are forced to practice defensive medicine. They order tests and write prescriptions that are not necessary, so they can protect themselves from trial lawyer lawsuits. One hospital CEO in New York said, "Fear of liability does nothing but threaten patient safety by discouraging open discussion of medical errors and ways to prevent them."

The total cost of defensive medicine to our society is estimated at $60 billion to $100 billion a year, and that includes $28 billion billed directly to the American taxpayers through increased costs of Medicare, Medicaid, Veterans Affairs, and other federal health programs. The costs of frivolous litigation are more than financial; they hurt patients all across America.

Most Americans are shocked when I cite the fact there are nearly 1,500 counties in the United States without an OB/GYN. We want our doctors focused on providing compassionate care, not fighting junk lawsuits. We want our hospitals pursuing innovative and promising ways to heal, not battling lawyers who second-guess them in the courts. This is a national issue that requires a national response. The House of Representatives have passed a good bill. The Senate has done nothing on medical liability reform. For the sake of affordable and accessible health care, we need medical liability reform this year.

I'm looking forward to working with the Congress to enact these reforms. This is a common-sense way of dealing with rising health care costs. And by dealing with rising health care costs, we will strengthen private medicine and fight off the calls of those in Washington, D.C. who want the federal government making all the decisions for health care.

The story of America's hospitals is a story of America's commitment to be a nation of care and compassion. America's strength and its goodness and prosperity is built on a trust in the extraordinary wisdom and power of the American people. And so I believe that by giving more Americans more control over their health care decisions, we will strengthen the doctor-patient relationship, and we will preserve the system of private medicine that has made our nation's hospitals and health care the best in the world.

People here in Washington need to trust the people. People here in Washington need to do common-sense things to address the rising costs of health care. And this person in Washington has come to thank you for your compassion and what you do for the communities all around America.

May God continue to bless your work, and may God bless our country. Thank you.

Health Care Justice in America

The Moral and Economic Imperatives to Cover the Uninsured

Risa Lavizzo-Mourey

President and CEO, Robert Wood Johnson Foundation, 2003– ; born Seattle, WA, September 25, 1954; University of Washington, 1972–73; State University of New York at Stony Brook, 1973–75; M.D., Harvard Medical School, 1979; M.B.A., Wharton School, University of Pennsylvania, 1986; medical resident, Brigham and Women's Hospital, Boston, 1979–82; clinical instructor, Temple University Medical School, Philadelphia, 1982–84; assistant professor of medicine, University of Pennsylvania School of Medicine, 1986–92; associate professor, University of Pennsylvania School of Medicine, 1992–97; Sylvan Eisman Professor of Medicine, University of Pennsylvania School of Medicine, 1997–2001; director, Institute of Aging, chief, Division of Geriatric Medicine, University of Pennsylvania School of Medicine, 1984–92, 1994–2001; associate chief of staff, Philadelphia Veterans' Administration Medical Center; deputy administrator, Agency for Health Care Policy and Research, Rockville, MD, 1992–94; senior vice president and director, Health Care Group, Robert Wood Johnson Foundation, 2001–02.

Editor's introduction: As the president and CEO of the Robert Wood Johnson Foundation, the nation's largest philanthropy devoted exclusively to improving health and health care, Risa Lavizzo-Mourey has worked to foster patient-centered health care and to deal with the growing ranks of the uninsured in the United States. She attributes her interest in public health and philanthropy to her parents—both of whom were physicians. "They inspired me from an early age to pursue a career in medicine and to think of myself as being the kind of person who wanted to help patients, one patient at a time," she told a reporter for *Philanthropy News Digest* (May 31, 2005). In the following speech, delivered as the Arthur Bachmeyer Memorial Address at the 50th Congress of the American College of Healthcare Executives (ACHE), she explains that improving the quality of the health care system "means changing systems and agendas so what you do and how you do it is driven not by what your process demands but by what your patients need."

Delivered on March 19, 2007, at New Orleans, LA. Used with permission from the Robert Wood Johnson Foundation in Princeton, New Jersey. *Copyright 2007 Robert Wood Johnson Foundation.*

Risa Lavizzo-Mourey's speech: Your 50th Congress! This is a big deal. You're not merely an organization, you are an institution. One that's trusted, relied upon and counted on.

The Bachmeyer Memorial is an institution in its own right, too. Looking back, the Bachmeyer annals are a running commentary on the past half century of health care in America.

I am honored and excited to make my own small contribution because this is such an historic moment for the future of patient care and how we deliver it in America.

Yours is a powerful voice in the debate over what that future is going to look like. I am here to encourage you to use that voice.

And I want to share with you our sense of the challenges, the promises and the rewards on the path before us, and how much we're going to count on your leadership to get us there.

From our perspective, it's all about the patient: medicine, margin, mission—the patient's always at the center.

Improving the quality of health care is our paramount priority, which means changing systems and agendas so what you do and how you do it is driven not by what your process demands but by what your patients need.

Patient-centered care: This means making sure that every man, woman and child in America has health coverage, especially our children.

By the time this day is over, if there is only one thing I've said that you still remember, this is what I want it to be:

That nothing in health care is more important than covering all the uninsured so that the care you provide is centered on all of us and not just on some of us.

Nothing is more important than this. I come to you as physician and as philanthropist. As a physician, I simply pull on my white lab coat, pick up a stethoscope, sit down in front of a real patient and ask, "OK, so tell me—what's bothering you."

But as a philanthropist charged with improving health and health care, that solitary patient is a part or a larger population of many—maybe even millions—of patients.

It's like going from singular to plural. But it's still the patient, plural and individual, that matters most.

As physician, as philanthropist, as an unabashed policy wonk, even as a patient myself, I've seen medicine and health care from every which way.

In the early 1990s I was one of those people up in Washington working to come up with the ideal health care system. We aspired to find all the answers. Instead, we learned that good intentions and grand schemes on their own are not enough to get the job done.

Just this morning, the new president of the American Hospital Association told us that if anyone has any chance of getting health care out of the fix it's in, first we have to listen and listen hard.

I think that's exactly what America's been doing—listening—to the data, to the providers, to the experiences of their own families. Lessons come to us in daily experiences.

For example, I'm on the Board of the Princeton Health-Care System. It's a real-world proving ground for all that's magnificent and all that's mortifying about health care today.

The lessons have amplified my hearing and magnified my vision—and I can tell you absolutely that your pain is now my pain.

Like you, we feel the tremendous tug-of-war between rising costs and never enough revenue; the uncertain fortunes of Medicare and Medicaid; the rocky relations between hospitals, health systems and physicians; and the monster difficulties of caring for the millions of our own families and neighbors who lack health insurance of any kind.

We have about 47 million uninsured, about 16 percent of our entire population, including 9 million children.

They pay a big price for being left out. The Institute of Medicine reports that some 18,000 die prematurely each year because they have no health insurance.

That's like having September 11 recur six times over every year, year after year.

We funded that report. In it, the IOM concluded that uninsured Americans are more likely to receive too little medical care, and when they do get it, too often it's too late.

They receive poorer care when they're in the hospital—even in a terrible emergency like a car crash. Ultimately, the uninsured live sicker and die sooner.

The evidence is all around us. Even before Katrina, nearly 12 percent of all the children in Louisiana were uninsured. That's almost 140,000 kids, plus three-quarter of a million adults.

Then came the whirlwind and a flood of biblical proportions.

Amidst the wreckage and suffering, the New Orleans health care landscape was horribly scarred, perhaps forever. For the uninsured, it was the worst possible thing that could happen.

Now it's a year and a half later. More than half the population of Orleans Parish is gone, maybe forever. Of those still here, twice as many are uninsured as before—as many as 50 percent of all adults under 65.

Meanwhile, the health care system itself was depopulated: The number of safety-net clinics fell from 90 to 19. The number of emergency medical units fell from 17 to 7. Hospital-staffed bed capacity fell fivefold. The number of available doctors fell from about 4,500 to 1,200.

At least 50 percent of all remaining kids have been without access to a primary care physician ever since. Thousands of uninsured pregnant women haven't been able to get prenatal care. Hospitals report a surge in premature and low birth weight babies. And last week local health officials told Congress that the number of deaths is up 40 percent from before the storm.

This is health care disaster writ as large as we've ever known.

Doctor Cathi Fontenot is the medical director of the Medical Center of Louisiana at New Orleans. That includes Charity Hospital—for 250 years a sanctuary for patients in need—and still closed.

Last Tuesday (March 13, 2007) Dr. Fontenot testified to Congress that the health care infrastructure in New Orleans "is tenuous and critically ill."

The uninsured are at the very eye of this storm within the storm.

New Orleans is a metaphor for how perilous health care in America has become. The shame of it is that our public leaders can't—or won't—agree on how best to care for the uninsured.

As a result, you're caught in the middle. The uninsured are right there with you.

The uncompensated care hospitals provide is awesome—nearly $30 billion a year. About half of all hospitals report their emergency departments are "at" or "over" capacity. Ambulance diversions are routine. So are shortages of on-call specialty physicians.

Medicaid and Medicare reimbursements are on the bubble. And the financial "margin" many of you are mandated to meet gets more elusive every year.

In New Jersey, where we live, 51 percent of our hospitals are in the red.

Yes, a great dark shadow has fallen across the social, clinical, and fiscal geography of health care in America—a shadow cast by the mass of millions of children and adults without health insurance.

We've been living under this shadow for so long and we've become so used to it that the appalling has become acceptable and this new "acceptable" we now consider "normal."

Can we escape the shadow? We can always hope.

Listen to what the President said: "Of all our national resources, none is of more basic value than the health of our people." He proposed "to provide adequate medical care to all who need it, not as charity but on the basis of payments made by the beneficiaries of the program."

That's what the President said, all right. But it wasn't President Bush. It wasn't even President Clinton. No, that was President Truman in 1947. That's when he asked Congress to approve universal health care coverage.

Sixty years and we're still waiting. And while we've waited;

- We've conquered killer diseases like polio and smallpox.

- We've unlocked life-giving mysteries of the human genome.

- Our life expectancy from birth increased from 68 to 78 years.

- We've even landed men on the moon and beamed video back from Mars.

But back down home in America we still haven't been able to guarantee that everyone in our society has access to affordable, decent health care. It occurs to me—if this was rocket science we wouldn't be in this mess.

This is all about to change. I'm not a politician or a pundit, but it seems to this physician that health system reform is making a political comeback. The evidence sure says so.

The latest public opinion polls report that the great majority of Americans—72 percent—do not approve of the way the government is handling health care. And as many as 64 percent now believe the federal government should guarantee health insurance for every American.

Only the war in Iraq ranks higher as an urgent national priority. This is the strongest level of public concern about any health care issue we've seen. It's almost 10 points higher than the Clinton plan's most popular moment 13 years ago.

What's stunned politicians and policymakers is that some 60 percent are willing to pay higher taxes to make it happen. That's a commanding 6 out of 10 people surveyed.

We've never seen motivation like this before. For the first time since Harry Truman, the great majority "gets it"—that the epidemic of un-insurance threatens all of us and not just some of us.

Katrina was the last straw. Two big lessons emerge from the chaos of the storm.

Lesson Number One: Katrina exposed an unforgiving and long-avoided truth: That mainstream America fails to regard huge numbers of our youngest and our oldest, our poorest and our sickest nonwhite people and their families as equal members of our society.

If you have any doubt whatsoever that we are defaulting to a two-tier society of haves and have-nots, just think of the lost and forgotten we saw on TV, huddled on their rooftops, clutching signs begging "HELP US," and calling out for food and water and care that did not come.

As we enjoy this lovely luncheon in this luxurious setting—do not forget that this was the reality within sight of this hotel.

That leads to Lesson Number Two: Most Americans presume they are among the "haves." They take it for granted that our government and institutions will secure their safety and protect their health when the time comes.

But when these expectations are not met, the American people get shocked. Then we get confused. Then we get mad as hell.

Down deep each of knows that but for the grace of God that could have been any of us out there on those rooftops.

Now we want answers. We want action. We want to do the right thing—right now!

I hear it every day, this great and honest desire among decent people everywhere to make life better, to care for our kids and families and to close the gap between the haves and have-nots so none of us are ever stranded in the flood again.

This is why the majority of Americans are ready to make sacrifices of their own to cover the uninsured. They're waking up to the fact that they very well could be the next in line.

A provocative new book on health care comes out next month. It's called *Sick*, it's by Jonathon Cohn, and it weaves together health care experiences of ordinary Americans with the history of the health system itself.

Cohn tells the story of Gary and Betsy Rotzler and their truly all-American family. High school sweethearts, college graduates, parents of two girls and a boy. The family lived not far from Cooperstown and Baseball's Hall of Fame.

Gary and Betsy were as traditional as it gets. One of Gary's ancestors was on the ship right behind the Mayflower. Betsy was a Girl Scout leader and made Raggedy-Ann dolls for family and friends.

Gary was an engineer for a defense contractor—until the Pentagon cut the funding and the contractor cut Gary. By the time Gary was rehired, the company no longer offered benefits.

Suddenly the Rotzlers, a family just like yours and mine, were among the millions of families without coverage. Betsy began putting off regular medical exams, despite her chronic fatigue and back pain.

Gary later realized that Betsy feared the worst and didn't want to bankrupt the family. By the time the cancer was diagnosed it didn't make any difference. Within days, Betsy fell into a coma.

At the hospital that last night, Gary stepped away to sign some forms. One was a promise to pay all the medical bills. By the time he got back to the room, the kids were arriving with "Get Well" balloons. But Betsy was gone, leaving behind a grief-stricken family and tens of thousands of dollars of debt.

This is what happens when health care is a privilege for those who can afford it and a Category 5 catastrophe when they cannot.

Gary recalled what it felt like. "When you walk into a doctor's office," he said, "and you've got to say you don't have insurance there is a mood swing, there is a change, no matter how nice that person is behind the desk. You're a different class of person."

We all know what this means. If it can happen to Betsy and Gary, it can happen to you. It can happen to me. It can happen to any of us—and it already is.

Forty-five percent of the public say they've been without health coverage at one time or another. That's almost half the population. The issue's felt across the kitchen tables of America.

Congressional insiders—Republican and Democrat—expect health care will get more attention in the 2008 campaign than any other issue than Iraq. "No candidate will be elected who does not have a specific health care proposal," one member of Congress said.

That's a 180-degree change from when we began our cover the uninsured campaign eight years ago. The problem wasn't even on the national radar screen. We wanted to move the needle but we couldn't even find the needle!

We needed help. We figured that if we could get the big stakeholders, even those with opposing points of view, to work together maybe we'd have a chance to cover the uninsured.

These were heavy hitters. The Chamber of Commerce and the AFL-CIO; the AMA and the big insurers; hospital groups like the AHA and CHA; health plans, advocacy groups and AARP.

They understood that the public sector stood frozen in the political headlights. And they understood that the only way to get them to blink would be for these tough characters from the private sector to take it right to the public sector.

Many of our partners are ideological and political adversaries and fierce competitors for the same shrinking health care dollar—and they still are. The media jokingly call them the "strange bedfellows coalition." They still are.

Some of you were there and know exactly what I mean. Getting this crowd together at the same time in the same place and keeping them there is like "herding cats."

Our aim is to create the climate in which these powerful stakeholders could find common ground and begin to take actions that as a philanthropy we cannot. Our strategy is both top-down and bottom-up, with effective advertising to drive it home.

We concentrate on an annual set of events this time of year called Cover the Uninsured Week. Hundreds of thousands have participated. It's become an annual health care rite of spring.

Remember all those town hall meetings and press conferences and health fairs out on the hospital front lawn? Thanks to you, it's finally paying off.

The private sector's now standing on common ground where the political sector so far has feared to tread, with notable exceptions like last year's accord in Massachusetts.

For the past couple of years many of our original partners have collaborated behind the scenes. They call themselves the "Health Coverage Coalition for the Uninsured."

They speak for much of the hospital and health care industries. They see that our old-time system of private employer health coverage is collapsing—perhaps for good.

Last week in Washington, we released research that shows it's harder and harder for working parents with lower incomes to obtain coverage for their kids—a 9 percent drop. Employer health insurance for lower-income workers has fallen at a rate triple that of wealthier workers.

Nationally, an average of 66 percent of children in low-income working families are uninsured. These families are doubly squeezed. They earn too much to qualify for Medicaid and too little to afford their own coverage.

For many, SCHIP may well be the only safety net left for their kids. SCHIP is the State Children's Health insurance Program. It's 10 years old—and up for reauthorization.

This may be the most significant vote on any domestic issue this Congress takes, partly because SCHIP is considered the trigger for broader changes in health care.

Beltway insiders say that SCHIP is a "bellwether" of what Congress is able to do on health.

Every one of you has a stake in the outcome. That's why the Health Coverage Coalition isn't waiting for someone else to act. On January 18 they announced a detailed proposal to expand health coverage, starting immediately with children.

This is huge. Here we have hospitals and health plans, doctors, the insurers, business, drug manufacturers and consumers, all under the same big tent, backed by massive public support, all saying to Washington in one voice: "If you won't lead, we will. Here's our plan for what you need to do. It starts with covering the kids."

We're not waiting, either. We tailored next month's Cover the Uninsured Week to build support for SCHIP. We begin Monday, April 23.

The case for SCHIP is compelling. SCHIP covers 6 million children. They get access to care they deserve and the recommended care they need.

Hospitals and clinics benefit along with the kids. In Texas, the percent of children using the ED [Emergency Department] as their main source of care fell from 20 to 2 percent. In Florida, children's visits to EDs dropped as much as 70 percent. This is good news.

But another 9 million kids are not covered. That's nearly 12 percent of all the children in the country. SCHIP and the states can't keep up without congressional action.

You need to let them know that the longer these kids are uninsured, the more drastically the trajectories of their lives are altered.

Uninsured children are:

- 10 times less likely to have a "medical home" and routine primary care.

- They're far less likely to get preventive care. Forty-eight percent never even get a well-child checkup.

- They're one and a half times more likely to miss hearing and vision screening.

- They forgo prescription drugs and treatment for illness or injury.

- They're four times more likely to end up in one of your emergency departments with conditions that could've been avoided.

- Uninsured kids are 25 percent more likely to miss school, especially if they have untreated chronic conditions.

- In some schools, uninsured kids are banned from sports programs.

Think about it: How many budding Bill Gateses or Michael Jordans do we lose because they're kids with no coverage?

How do we answer a question like that? What's gone so terribly wrong that we even have to ask it? Is it because we don't care? Of course we care. Is it because we don't know what to do? Of course we know what to do. Is it because we lack resources? Of course we have the resources.

Why, then, have we allowed the appalling to become the acceptable, putting our children at such high risk? We could spend the rest of this meeting and we still wouldn't get through all the possible explanations.

Let me suggest this: We haven't taken the time to connect the dots between: One, the uninsured; Two, the quality of care; and Three, the economics of health care.

Let's start with some basic precepts. Call them Risa's Principles of Care for Everyone.

My First Principle—Health care is a human right. It is not negotiable.

Second—Guaranteeing everyone access to affordable quality care is a moral and economic imperative.

Third—The cost of coverage is an obligation shared by the three guarantors of the great social contract that binds all of us together.

These guarantors are:

- The individual. That's each of us.

- Next: Our government—of, for and by the people. Not the politicians, not the special interests, but all of us working together for our common good.

- The private sector is the final guarantor. That's most of us here. Securing social value is as necessary as securing shareholder value.

The only way to connect the dots of coverage, quality and economy is to keep this social contract and its three guarantors in equilibrium. Our system worked well for a long time. Now, though, it's changing—and not for the better.

Jonathon Cohn says we're going backward—not forward. Instead of individuals being drawn together in mutual health care defense systems, we're being cast adrift, like the Rotzlers.

Fewer employers offer health benefits. Insurers don't want anything to do with people with chronic medical conditions. The prospectively sick, the vulnerable, children, families on the bubble—one by one they're stranded to face greater and greater risks on their own.

As for providers—including hospitals—no one is thrilled when caring for the uninsured diverts their resources from their paying customers. Health care's a commodity and selling it is so profitable, no one wants to foot the bill for health care's equivalent of a free lunch.

Meanwhile, high-cost premiums are out of the reach of too many working people. What coverage they can afford buys false security— and not much else.

And how can we trust our public programs? Just when our population's getting older, Medicare's well is drying up. The governors warn that Medicaid's being gutted.

Our public programs—including the public health infrastructure—are plagued by fiscal anemia, political expedience and ideological tampering.

Somewhere in this cold-cash process of exclusion and political calculation, health care for millions of us became an indulgence that's accessible if you can afford it and isn't accessible if you can't.

That's bad public policy, bad medical policy and bad economic policy.

Here's where we connect those dots. First, we need a serious attitude adjustment. I'm glad you're sitting down—because I have to tell you that change is not all about the money.

Cutting spending in the short-term will not cure what ails health care. Remember the promise of managed care? No, change is all about changing systems of patient care and not just systems of cost control.

As the IOM tells us, change is not about doing more, charging more, working more. Change is about doing better. And we cannot do better until we cover the uninsured.

We believe that when everyone has coverage, we will find a new reality of improvements in care, costs, consequences, even in compensation.

These are the promises and rewards of covering the uninsured:

- We will flourish in a system of quality care that's accessible and affordable for everyone.

- Patients will be full-fledged partners in their own care—and you'll actually be glad to see them there.

- Conducting the business of care will be easier and more rewarding.

- That daunting demand for uncompensated care that's costing you billions a year will diminish as the health of individuals and communities improves.

- Cost-shifting will ease, insurance premiums will lessen, and the taxpayer's burden will be lighter.

- We'll finally be able to identify, measure and reward quality performance—once the weight and shadow of the uninsured no longer skew the numbers and the outcomes.

- The system will be honest, open, transparent—and accountable.

- Consumers will take in the new data and make better decisions when they go medical shopping.

- We'll know for the first time how to truly deliver the best possible care with the highest possible value for the dollar.

- Hospitals will be full of high tech, ERs will be capable of handling each day's surge of patients—and they'll all be covered!

- As you unlock the secrets of doing better you'll have more revenue to invest in higher quality performance, which will produce more revenue.

- And in Washington, at long last the lions of the marketplace will sit down with what so far have been the lambs of the public sector—and openly and honestly collaborate with the American people to make health care available to everyone who needs it, when they need it, at a price we can all afford, and with the quality that we all deserve.

It's so close I can almost taste it!

Your role as America's health care executives will be determinative. It starts where you live and what you do and where you work every day.

It's no secret that the public thinks health care's mostly a profit-driven supplier of a commercial commodity—whether you're for-profit or not.

For generations, the public assumed health care institutions were putting value back into society and fighting for the good health of patients and communities. Now many believe you are more corporate than caring. When they see you falling short of their expectations they stop trusting you.

You have the power to change all that—if you have the courage to change as well.

We stand on the threshold of a rare moment in the history of American health care.

If we work together to cover the uninsured we will be creating a healthier future. But if we stumble over our own narrow vision and vested interests, we'll perpetuate a status quo that's appalling and unacceptable.

Trust me: This moment will be fleeting. I urge you: Don't wait for Washington to act. Demand from Congress and our candidates that they'd better have a credible plan out there if they want our vote. And demand their pledge to live up to their plan.

There is more that you can do:

Be leaders yourselves. Convene the players in your orbit—providers, insurers, government, philanthropies, patients and the public. Promote approaches and partnerships with other providers. Motivate and mobilize grassroots stakeholders and advocates.

Take your message to the media. Be out front, visible, vocal, and publicly accountable. Speak out—for the uninsured, for patient safety, for quality care and for the well-being of your entire community, be it local or national.

Seize the attention of local, state and federal lawmakers. Hold their feet to the fire and their honor answerable for covering the uninsured. If they fail to act—hold them accountable for that, too.

In other words, return to your roots. Be who you say you are—concerned, compassionate and committed. Prove to your own constituents that your mission is broader than your margin, that your bottom line includes covering the uninsured and improving the health of the community.

Always remember: You are a major guarantor of the American social contract. And know this: The rest of us are counting on you to help make all this work.

It's been said that justice is the first requisite of civilization. And that if we do not maintain and preserve justice, justice will not maintain and preserve us.

We won't have health justice in America until we cover all the uninsured. We won't close the gap between the haves and have-nots until we cover the uninsured.

The moral, economic and political imperatives command that we act now and we act together.

When we do—for the first time in the life of our Republic our society will enjoy true health care equality. Then we can rest—assured that we have met the just and the first requisite of our civilization and that justice is maintaining and preserving all Americans and the good health of all America.

Cutting Costs and Covering America

A 21st Century Health Care System

Barack Obama

U.S. senator (D), Illinois, 2005– ; born Honolulu, HI, August 4, 1961; early education in Jakarta, Indonesia, and Honolulu; B.A., Columbia University, 1983; J.D., Harvard Law School, 1992; first African-American president of the Harvard Law Review; *community organizer and civil rights lawyer in Chicago; senior lecturer, University of Chicago Law School, specializing in constitutional law; state senator, representing the South Side of Chicago, Illinois State Senate, 1997–2004; elected to U.S. Senate, 2004; U.S. Senate committees: Environment & Public Works, Foreign Relations, and Veterans' Affairs; organizations: Center for Neighborhood and Technology, Chicago Annebery Challenge, Cook County Bar, Community Law Project, Joyce Foundation, Lawyers' Committee for Civil Rights Under the Law, Leadership for Quality Education, Trinity United Church of Christ; award, 40 under 40, Crains Chicago Business, 1993; author,* Dreams from My Father: A Story of Race and Inheritance *(1995, reprinted 2004);* The Audacity of Hope: Thoughts on Reclaiming the American Dream *(2006).*

Editor's introduction: Nearly all of the Democratic presidential hopefuls have made health care reform central to their campaigns. The plan that Senator Barack Obama has offered would retain the private insurance system but expand coverage to more Americans—though, unlike the proposal offered by fellow Democratic presidential candidate John Edwards, it falls short of universal coverage. Under Obama's initiative, which mirrors that offered to members of Congress, those who cannot afford insurance on their own would receive a government subsidy. In this speech, which he delivered at the Univeristy of Iowa, Obama outlines his vision of national health care.

Barack Obama's speech: I want to thank the University of Iowa for having us here, and I want to give a special thanks to Amy and Lane for joining me today to tell their story.

A few hours north of here, Amy and Lane run a small business that offers internet service to their community. They were the very first company to provide broadband access in their remote corner of northeastern Iowa, and every day, hundreds of people count on the services they provide to do their jobs and live their lives.

But today they are on the brink of bankruptcy—a bankruptcy that has nothing to do with any poor business decision they made or slump in the economy they weren't prepared for.

Delivered on May 29, 2007, at Iowa City, IA.

Lane was diagnosed with cancer when he was twenty-one years old. He lost a lung, a leg bone and part of a hip. Seventeen years later, he is cancer-free, but the cost of health insurance for him, his wife and his three kids is now over $1,000 per month. Their family's premiums keep rising hundreds of dollars every year, and as hard as they look, they simply cannot find another provider that will insure them.

Amy and Lane are now paying forty percent of their annual income in health care premiums. They have no retirement plan and nothing saved. They can no longer afford to buy new clothes or fill up their cars with gas, they have racked up more credit card debt then they know what to do with, and Amy wrote to us and said that the day she heard the loan officer say the word "bankruptcy" was one of the worst in her life.

"My heart was in pain," she said. "This is not who we are. We have done everything right. We have done everything we were supposed to do. This is not who we are."

Amy is right. This is not who we are. We are not a country that rewards hard work and perseverance with bankruptcies and foreclosures. We are not a country that allows major challenges to go unsolved and unaddressed while our people suffer needlessly. In the richest nation on Earth, it is simply not right that the skyrocketing profits of the drug and insurance industries are paid for by the skyrocketing premiums that come from the pockets of the American people.

> We are not a country that rewards hard work and perseverance with bankruptcies and foreclosures.

This is not who we are. And this is not who we have to be.

In the past few months, I've heard stories like Amy's at town halls we've held in New Hampshire, and here in Iowa, and all across the country. Stories from people who are hanging on by a thread because of the stack of medical bills they can't pay. People who don't know where else to turn for help, but who do know that when it comes to health care, we have talked, tinkered, and let this crisis fester for decades. People who watch as every year, candidates offer up detailed health care plans with great fanfare and promise, only to see them crushed under the weight of Washington politics and drug and insurance industry lobbying once the campaign is over.

Well this cannot be one of those years. We have reached a point in this country where the rising cost of health care has put too many families and businesses on a collision course with financial ruin and left too many without coverage at all; a course that Democrats and Republicans, small business owners and CEOs have all come to agree is not sustainable or acceptable any longer.

We often hear the statistic that there are 45 million uninsured Americans. But the biggest reason why they don't have insurance is the same reason why those who do have it are struggling to pay their medical bills—it's just too expensive.

Health care premiums have risen nearly 90% in the past six years. That's four times faster than wages have gone up. Like Amy and Lane's family, nearly half of all Iowans have said that they've had to cut back on food and heating expenses because of high health care costs. 11 million insured Americans spent more than a quarter of their salary on health care last year. And over half of all personal bankruptcies are now caused by medical bills.

Businesses aren't faring much better. Over half of all small businesses can no longer afford to insure their workers, and so many others have responded to rising costs by laying off workers or shutting their doors for good. Some of the biggest corporations in America, giants of industry like GM and Ford, are watching foreign competitors based in countries with universal health care run circles around them, with a GM car containing seven times as much health care cost as a Japanese car.

This cost crisis is trapping us in a vicious cycle. As premiums rise, more employers drop coverage, and more Americans become uninsured. Every time those uninsured walk into an emergency room and receive care that's more expensive because they have nowhere else to turn, there is a hidden tax for the rest of us as premiums go up by an extra $922 per family. And as premiums keep rising, more families and businesses drop their coverage and become uninsured.

It would be one thing if all this money we spend on premiums and co-payments and deductibles went directly towards making us healthier and improving the quality of our care.

But it doesn't. One out of every four dollars we spend on health care is swallowed up by administrative costs—on needless paperwork and antiquated record-keeping that belongs in the last century. This failure to update the way our doctors and hospitals store and share information also leads to costly errors. Each year, 100,000 Americans die due to medical errors and we lose $100 billion because of prescription drug errors alone.

We also spend far more on treating illnesses and conditions that could've been prevented or managed for far less. Our health care system is turning into a disease care system, where too many plans and providers don't offer or encourage check-ups and tests and screenings that could save thousands of lives and billions of dollars down the road.

Of course, the biggest obstacle in the way of reforming this skewed system of needless waste and spiraling costs are those who profit most from the status quo—the drug and insurance companies who pocket a growing chunk of the medical bills that people like Amy and Lane are going bankrupt trying to pay.

Since President Bush took office, the single fastest growing component of health care spending has been administrative costs and profits for insurance companies. Coming in a close second is the amount we spend on prescription drugs. In 2006, five of the biggest drug and insurance companies were among the fifty most profitable businesses in the nation. One insurance company CEO received a $125 million salary that same year, and has been given stock options worth over $1 billion. As an added perk, he and his wife get free private health care for as long as they live.

Now, making this kind of money costs money, which is why the drug and insurance industries have also spent more than $1 billion on lobbying and campaign contributions over the last ten years to block the kind of reform we need. They've been pretty good at it too, preventing the sale of cheaper prescription drugs and defeating attempts to make it harder for insurance companies to deny coverage on the basis of a preexisting condition.

Look, it's perfectly understandable for a business to try and make a profit, and every American has the right to make their case to the people who represent us in Washington.

But I also believe that every American has the right to affordable health care. I believe that the millions of Americans who can't take their children to a doctor when they get sick have that right. I believe that people like Amy and Lane who are on the brink of losing everything they own have that right. And I believe that no amount of industry profiteering and lobbying should stand in the way of that right any longer.

That's not who we are.

We now face an opportunity—and an obligation—to turn the page on the failed politics of yesterday's health care debates. It's time to bring together businesses, the medical community, and members of both parties around a comprehensive solution to this crisis, and it's time to let the drug and insurance industries know that while they'll get a seat at the table, they don't get to buy every chair.

We can do this. The climate is far different than it was the last time we tried this in the early nineties. Since then, rising costs have caused many more businesses to back reform, and in states from Massachusetts to California, Democratic and Republican governors and legislatures have been way ahead of Washington in passing increasingly bolder initiatives to cover the uninsured and cut costs.

We've had some success in Illinois as well. As a state senator, I brought Republicans and Democrats together to pass legislation insuring 20,000 more children and 65,000 more parents. I authored and passed a bill cracking down on hospital price gouging of uninsured patients, and helped expand coverage for routine mammograms for women on Medicaid. We created hospital report cards, so that every consumer could see things like the ratio of nurses to patients, the number of annual medical errors, and the quality of care they could expect at each hospital. And I passed a law that put Illinois on a path to universal coverage.

It's a goal I believe we can achieve on a national level with the health care plan I'm outlining today. The very first promise I made on this campaign was that as president, I will sign a universal health care plan into law by the end of my first term in office. Today I want to lay out the details of that plan—a plan that not only guarantees coverage for every American, but also brings down the cost of health care and reduces every family's premiums by as much as $2500. This second part is important because, in the end, coverage without cost containment will only shift our burdens, not relieve them. So we will take steps to remove the waste and inefficiency from the system so we can bring down costs and improve the quality of our care while we're at it.

My plan begins by covering every American.

If you already have health insurance, the only thing that will change for you under this plan is the amount of money you will spend on premiums. That will be less.

If you are one of the 45 million Americans who don't have health insurance, you will have it after this plan becomes law. No one will be turned away because of a preexisting condition or illness. Everyone will be able buy into a new health insurance plan that's similar to the one that every federal employee—from a postal worker in Iowa to a Congressman in Washington—currently has for themselves. It will cover all essential medical services, including preventive, maternity, disease management, and mental health care. And it will also include high standards for quality and efficiency.

If you cannot afford this insurance, you will receive a subsidy to pay for it. If you have children, they will be covered. If you change jobs, your insurance will go with you. If you need to see a doctor, you will not have to wait in long lines for one. If you want more choices, you will also have the option of purchasing a number of affordable private plans that have similar benefits and standards for quality and efficiency.

To help pay for this, we will ask all but the smallest businesses who don't make a meaningful contribution today to the health coverage of their employees to do so by supporting this new plan. And we will allow the temporary Bush tax cut for the wealthiest Americans to expire.

But we also have to demand greater efficiencies from our health care system. Today, we pay almost twice as much for health care per person than other industrialized nations, and too much of it has nothing to do with patient care.

That's why the second part of my health care plan includes five, long-overdue steps we will take to bring down costs and bring our health care system into the 21st century—steps that will save each American family up to $2500 on their premiums.

First, we will reduce costs for business and their workers by picking up the tab for some of the most expensive illnesses and conditions.

Right now, two out of every ten patients account for more than eighty percent of all health care costs. These are patients with serious illnesses like cancer or heart disease who require the most expensive surgeries and treatments. Insurance companies end up spending a lion's share of their expenses on these patients, and not surprisingly, they pass those expenses on to the rest of us in the

form of higher premiums. Under my proposal, the federal government will pay for part of these catastrophic cases, which means that
your premiums will go down.

Second, we will finally begin focusing our health care system on
preventing costly, debilitating conditions in the first place.

We all know the saying that an ounce of prevention is worth a
pound of cure. But today we're nowhere close to that ounce. We
spend less than four cents of every health care dollar on prevention
and public health even though eighty percent of the risk factors
involved in the leading causes of death are behavior-related and
thus preventable.

The problem is, there's currently no financial incentive for health
care providers to offer services that will encourage patients to eat
right or exercise or go for annual check-ups and screenings that can
help detect diseases early. The real profit today is made in treating
diseases, not preventing them. That's wrong, which is why in our
new national health care plan and other participating plans, we will
require coverage of evidence-based, preventive care services, and
make sure they are paid for.

But in the end, prevention only works if we take responsibility for
our own health and make the right decisions in our own lives—if we
eat the right foods, and stay active, and listen to our wives when
they tell us to stop smoking.

Third, we will reduce the cost of our health care by improving the
quality of our health care.

It's estimated that poor quality care currently costs us up to $100
billion a year. One study found that in Pennsylvania, Medicare
spent $1 billion a year just on treating infections that patients con-
tracted while at the hospital—infections that could have easily been
prevented by hospitals. This study led hospitals across the state to
take action, and today some have completely eliminated infections
that used to take hundreds of lives and cost hundreds of thousands
of dollars every year.

Much like the hospital report cards we passed in Illinois, my
health care proposal will ask hospitals and providers to collect,
track, and publicly report measures of health care quality. We'll provide the public with information about preventable medical errors,
nurse-to-patient ratios, and hospital-acquired infections. We'll also
start measuring what's effective and what's not when it comes to
different drugs and procedures, so that patients can finally start
making informed choices about the care that's best for them. And
instead of rewarding providers and physicians only by the sheer
quantity of services and procedures they prescribe, we'll start
rewarding them for the quality of the outcomes for their patients.

Fourth, we will reduce waste and inefficiency by moving from a
20th century health care industry based on pen and paper to a 21st
century industry based on the latest information technology.

Almost every other industry in the world has saved billions on administrative costs by computerizing all of their records and information. Every transaction you make at a bank now costs less than a dollar. Even at the Veterans Administration, where it used to cost nine dollars to pull up your medical record, new technology means you can call up the same record on the internet for next to nothing.

But because we haven't updated technology in the rest of the health care industry, a single transaction still costs up to twenty-five dollars.

This reform is long overdue. By moving to electronic medical records, we can give doctors and nurses easy access to all the necessary information about their patients, so if they type-in a certain prescription, a patient's allergies will pop right up on the screen. This will reduce deadly medical errors, and it will also shorten the length of hospital stays, ensure that nurses can spend less time on paperwork and more time with patients, and save billions and billions of dollars in the process.

> We will break the stranglehold that a few big drug and insurance companies have on the health care market.

Finally, we will break the stranglehold that a few big drug and insurance companies have on the health care market.

We all value the medical cures and innovations that the pharmaceutical industry has developed over the years, but it's become clear that some of these companies are dramatically overcharging Americans for what they offer. They'll sell the same exact drugs here in America for double the price of what they charge in Europe and Canada. They'll push expensive products on doctors by showering them with gifts, spend more to market and advertise their drugs than to research and develop them, and when a generic drug maker comes along and wants to sell the same product for cheaper, the brand-name manufacturers will actually payoff the generic ones so they can preserve their monopolies and keep charging the rest of us high prices.

We don't have to stand for that anymore. Under my plan, we will make generic drugs more available to consumers and we will tell the drug companies that their days of forcing affordable prescription drugs out of the market are over.

And it's not just the drug industry that's manipulating the market. In the last ten years, there have been over four hundred health insurance mergers. Right here in Iowa, just three companies control more than three-quarters of the health insurance market. These changes were supposed to increase efficiency in the industry. But what's really increased is the amount of money we're paying them.

This is wrong, and when I'm President, we're going to make drug and insurance companies compete for their customers just like every other business in America. We'll investigate and prosecute the monopolization of the insurance industry. And where we do find places where insurance companies aren't competitive, we will make them pay a reasonable share of their profits on the patients they should be caring for in the first place. Because that's what's right.

We are a country that looks at the thousands of stories just like Amy and Lane's—stories we have heard and told for decades—and realizes that our American story calls on us to write them a hopeful, happier ending. After all, that's what we've done before.

Half a century ago, America found itself in the midst of another health care crisis. For millions of elderly Americans, the single greatest cause of poverty and hardship was the crippling cost of their health care. A third of all elderly Americans lived in poverty, and nearly half had no health insurance.

As health care and hospital costs continued to rise, more and more private insurers simply refused to insure our elderly, believing they were too great of a risk to care for.

The resistance to action was fierce. Proponents of health care reform were opposed by well-financed, well-connected interest groups who spared no expense in telling the American people that these efforts were "dangerous" and "un-American," "revolutionary" and even "deadly."

And yet the reformers marched on. They testified before Congress and they took their case to the country and they introduced dozens of different proposals but always, always they stood firm on their goal to provide affordable health care for every American senior. And finally, after years of advocacy and negotiation and plenty of setbacks, President Lyndon Johnson signed the Medicare bill into law on July 30th of 1965.

The signing ceremony was held in Missouri, in a town called Independence, with the man who issued the call for universal health care during his own presidency—Harry Truman.

And as he stood with Truman by his side and signed what would become one of the most successful government programs in history—a program that had seemed impossible for so long—President Johnson looked out at the crowd and said, "History shapes men, but it is a necessary faith of leadership that men can help shape history."

Never forget that we have it within our power to shape history in this country. It is not in our character to sit idly by as victims of fate or circumstance, for we are a people of action and innovation, forever pushing the boundaries of what's possible.

Now is the time to push those boundaries once more. We have come so far in the debate on health care in this country, but now we must finally answer the call issued by Truman, advanced by Johnson, and pushed along by the simple power of stories like the one told by Amy and Lane. The time has come for affordable, universal health care in America. And I look forward to working with all of you to meet this challenge in the weeks and months to come. Thank you.

Speech at Des Moines Rotary Lunch

John McCain

U.S. senator (R), Arizona, 1987– ; born Panama Canal Zone, August 29, 1936; graduated United States Naval Academy, 1958; naval aviator, 1958–80; shot down over Vietnam, 1967, and held as prisoner-of-war in Hanoi, 1967–73; retired from the Navy as Captain, 1981; U.S. representative (R), Arizona's First District, 1983–87; elected to U.S. Senate, 1986; U.S. Senate committees: Armed Services (ranking member); Commerce, Science, and Transportation; and Indian Affairs; military honors include Silver Star, Bronze Star, Legion of Merit, Purple Heart, and Distinguished Flying Cross; named one of the "25 Most Influential People in America" by Time, *1997; author,* Faith of My Fathers: A Family Memoir, *2000.*

Editor's introduction: In the following speech, delivered before the Des Moines, IA, Rotary, Senator John McCain states that although Americans have "fine doctors, medical technology and treatments," health care costs are just too high for many people. In his proposed solution, the Republican presidential candidate stresses individual accountability. "Has any candidate warned that we have a personal responsibility to take better care of ourselves and our children?" he asks. Senator McCain's plan would create physician-coordinated health-care options for patients; allow insurance companies to sell health policies nationally instead of state-by-state; and provide tax credits for families and individuals. McCain calls his plan a "genuinely conservative vision for health care reform."

John McCain's speech: Thank you for the opportunity to talk today about the American health care system. You don't have to be a candidate for President to discover that worries over the availability and cost of health care trouble the waking hours and disturb the sleep of more Americans than any other single domestic issue. Indeed, outside of the pre-eminent challenge of our time—the threat of Islamic extremists—no issue comes up more frequently in large and small public discussions, in polls, debates and media reports.

So it is surely appropriate that the subject figures prominently in this presidential election. And in our eagerness to appear responsive to this acute public concern, every candidate will feel compelled to offer his or her "solution" to the problem. But will these solutions actually improve our health care system? Or will they merely serve as the candidates' opening ante in what looks to become a bidding war? In our haste will we promise more than we can deliver? Will we misdiagnose the problem and devise a cure that will kill the

Delivered on October 11, 2007, at Des Moines, IA.

patient? Will we even ask ourselves that first, most important of questions: what exactly is the problem with the American health care system?

The problem, my friends, is not that Americans don't have fine doctors, medical technology and treatments. The state of our medical science is the envy of the world. The problem is not that most Americans lack adequate health insurance. The vast majority of Americans have private insurance and our government spends billions each year to provide even more.

The biggest problem with the American health care system is that it costs too much, and the way inflationary pressures are actually built into it. Businesses and families pay more and more every year to get what they often consider to be inadequate attention or poor care. And those who want to buy insurance are often unable to because of the high cost. What more compelling evidence of the problem do we need than to note that General Motors now spends more for the health care of its employees and retirees than for the material required to manufacture its products—steel. The price of every GM car includes over $1500 for health care costs compared to Toyota, whose total cost for health care per car is about $200.

The growth of costs affects everyone: government overspending, business costs and family budgets. It hurts those who have insurance by making it more expensive to keep. And it hurts those who don't have insurance by making it even harder to attain.

We are approaching a "perfect storm" of problems that if not addressed by the next president, will cause our health care system to implode. Here is what we know: First, we currently spend 2.2 trillion dollars—16 cents of every dollar we spend—on health care. By 2015, just seven years from now, that number will nearly double to four trillion dollars. Second, by 2019 Medicare will be broke. We are currently spending more on Medicare than we are collecting in payroll taxes and cashing in the few IOU's left in the trust fund. In the meantime, more and more of our retirees' social security checks will also go to pay for Medicare, leaving our seniors with less money for their everyday expenses. Third, by 2017 more money will be going out of social security than is coming in. The next president must act to avert the impending "storm."

For all the grandiose promises made in this campaign, has any candidate spoken honestly to the American people about the government's role and failings about individual responsibilities? Has any candidate told the truth about the future of Medicare? Its costs are growing astronomically faster than its financing, and leaving its structural flaws unaddressed will hasten its bankruptcy. Has any candidate warned that we have a personal responsibility to take better care of ourselves and our children? Yet that is the only way to prevent many chronic diseases. Has any candidate insisted that genuine and effective health care reform requires accountability from everyone: drug companies, insurance companies, doctors, hospitals, the government and patients? Yet that is the truth upon which any so-called solution must be based.

Democratic presidential candidates are not telling you these truths. They offer their usual default position: if the government would only pay for insurance everything would be fine. They promise universal coverage, whatever its cost, and the massive tax increases, mandates and government regulation that it imposes.

I offer a genuinely conservative vision for health care reform, which preserves the most essential value of American lives—freedom. Conservatives believe in the pursuit of personal, political and economic freedom for everyone. We believe that free people may voluntarily unite, but cannot be compelled to do so, and that the limited government that results best protects our individual freedom. In health care, we believe in enhancing the freedom of individuals to receive necessary and desired care. We do not believe in coercion and the use of state power to mandate care, coverage or costs.

I believe Americans want to be part of a system that offers high quality care; that respects their individual dignity and is available at reasonable cost. Unfortunately, the American health care system as it is currently structured fails this test. It is too expensive. It insults our common sense and dignity with excessive paperwork, disconnected visits with too many specialists, and by elaborately hiding from us any clear idea of what we are getting for our money. We must reform the health care system to make it responsive to the needs of American families. Not the government. Not the insurance companies. Not tort lawyers. Not even the doctors and hospitals.

The next president will have to take on the special interests that thrive in the health care system. Doctors must do a better job of managing our care and keeping us healthy and out of hospitals and nursing homes. We will need alternatives to doctors' offices and emergency rooms. Hospitals must do a better job of taking care of us when we are there, commit far fewer deadly and costly medical errors and generally operate more efficiently. Pharmaceutical companies must worry less about squeezing additional profits from old medicines by copying the last successful drug and insisting on additional patent protections and focus more on new and innovative medicine. Insurance companies should spend more on medical care and less on "administration."

My reforms are built on the pursuit of three goals: paying only for quality medical care, having insurance choices that are diverse and responsive to individual needs, and restoring our sense of personal responsibility.

These reforms are also built on the most fundamental of medical tenets: do no harm. There is much to be admired about medicine in America, and I want to protect those qualities. Doctors and other providers want to provide quality care. Lower costs mean that Medicare premiums don't continue to spiral beyond our ability to sustain it, and our insurance premiums are stretched farther. Most importantly, any reform must respect the freedom to keep your care and insurance just as they are.

The first principal of real reform is that Americans should pay only for quality. Right now, too much of the system is built on getting paid just for providing services, regardless of whether those services are necessary or produce quality care and outcomes. American families should only pay for getting the right care: care that is intended to improve their health.

American families know quality when they see it, so their dollars should be in their hands. When families are informed about medical choices, they are more capable of making their own decisions, less likely to choose the most expensive and often unnecessary options, and are more satisfied with their choices. Health Savings Accounts are tax-preferred accounts used to pay insurance premiums and other health costs. They put the family in charge of what they pay for, and should be expanded and encouraged.

I am committed to ensuring the finest quality medical care for our veterans. They have earned that consideration and more. They should not have to wait for access to a VA facility that is hours away. We can give them the option to put the means for financing their care under their control—in an electronic card or other device—so that if they want they can choose their care in another way that suits them best.

> American families know quality when they see it, so their dollars should be in their hands.

We cannot let the search for high-quality care be derailed by frivolous lawsuits and excessive damage awards. We must pass medical liability reform, and those reforms should eliminate lawsuits for doctors that follow clinical guidelines and adhere to patient safety protocols. If the Democrats are sincere in their conviction that health care coverage and quality is their first priority, than they will put the needs of patients before the demands of trial lawyers. But they can't have it both ways.

Research shows that coordinated care—providers collaborating to produce the best health outcome—offers better quality and costs less. We should pay a single bill for high-quality heart care, not an endless series of bills for pre-surgical tests and visits, hospitalization and surgery, and follow-up tests, drugs and office visits. Paying for coordinated care means that every single provider is now united on being responsive to the needs of a single person: the patient. Health information technology will flourish because the market will demand it.

Clinics, hospitals, doctors, medical technology producers, drug companies and every other provider of health care must be accountable and their transactions transparent. Families, insurance companies, the government—whoever is paying the bill—must understand exactly what their care costs and the outcome they received.

Families place a high value on quickly getting simple care, and have shown a willingness to pay cash to get it. If walk-in clinics in retail outlets are the most convenient, cost-effective way for families to safely meet simple needs why should government stand in their way? I will not.

If the cheapest way to get high quality care is to use advances in web technology to allow a doctor to practice across state lines, then let them. In disasters like Katrina we saw how stupid and harmful it is to refuse the services of doctors just because they had an out-of-state address. We should have a national market place, and if I'm elected President, we will.

Drugs are an important part of medicine, of course, and are often quite expensive. Here in Iowa the Attorney General is suing seventy-eight drug companies accusing them of inflating drug costs paid by Iowa taxpayers through the Medicaid system. Problems with costs are created when market forces are replaced by government regulated prices. If drug costs reflects value, fine. But if there are ways to bring greater competition to our drug markets by safe re-importation of drugs, by faster introduction of generic drugs, or by any other means, we should do so. If I'm elected President, we will.

Government programs such as Medicare and Medicaid should lead the way in health care reforms that improve quality and lower costs. Like most of our system, Medicare reimbursement now rewards institutions and clinicians who provide more and more complex services. We need to change the way providers are paid to focus their attention more on chronic disease and managing their treatment. This is the most important care and expense for an aging population. And in a system that rewards quality, Medicare should not pay for preventable medical errors. I am appreciative of the therapeutic benefits of modern pharmaceuticals. However, I strongly opposed adding another unfunded entitlement to the fiscal train wreck that is Medicare by providing all seniors with a costly drug benefit, even those, like me, who can more than afford to pay for their medicine.

The second principle of effective reform is to have insurance choices so varied and responsive to individual needs that you could fire your insurance company if you wanted to. Right now, too many of our citizens don't have an insurance policy at all, and those who do are afraid they will lose the one they have—afraid they will get too sick, afraid to stay home and not work full-time, and afraid their benefits will disappear along with their job.

I believe that everyone should get a tax credit of $2500, $5000 for families, if they have health insurance. It is good tax policy to take away the bias toward giving workers benefits instead of wages. It is good health policy to reward having insurance no matter where your policy comes from.

To use their money effectively, Americans need more choices. We should give additional help to those who face particularly expensive care. If it is done right and the additional money is there, insurance companies will compete for these patients—not turn them away. It is a challenge to develop techniques that allocate the right amount to each of these families. I propose that we try a time-honored approach and let the states work on whatever method they find most promising. The federal government can help fund this effort, but in exchange, states should allow Medicaid and SCHIP funds to be used for private insurance and develop methods to augment Medicaid and tax credits for more expensive care.

Family-based policies translate into broad success when they are paired with greater competition among insurers on a level playing field. You should be able to buy your insurance from any willing provider—the state bureaucracies are no better than national ones. Nationwide insurance markets that ensure broad and vigorous competition will wring out excess costs, overhead, and bloated executive compensation. Introducing competition into the health insurance market will reduce costs.

Some are already content with the choices and advice offered by their employer. Fine. But Americans should be able to choose who they trust. If a church or professional organization wishes to sponsor insurance for its members, they should be able to do so.

When an American family controls its own health care financing, has a wide variety of low-cost, innovative choices, and receives insurance through a sponsor they trust, insurance policies will only disappear when the family decides it doesn't serve them as well as a competitor would.

The final important principle of reform is to rediscover our sense of personal responsibility. We must personally do everything we can to prevent expensive, chronic diseases. Our rights in this country are protected by our personal sense of responsibility for our own well being. Cases of diabetes are going up, not only in the baby boom generation, but among younger Americans obesity, diabetes and high blood pressure are all on the rise. Parents who don't impart to their children a sense of personal responsibility for their health, nutrition and exercise—vital quality of life information that political correctness has expelled from our schools—have failed their responsibility. Also, parents are responsible for ensuring that their children are covered by health insurance if, as is often the case, many options are already available to them.

We can build a health care system that is more responsive to our needs and is delivered to more people at lower cost. The "solution," my friends, isn't a one-size-fits-all big government takeover of health care. It resides where every important social advance has always resided—with the American people themselves, with well informed American families, making practical decisions to address their imperatives for better health and more secure prosperity. The engine of our prosperity and progress has always been our freedom and the sense of responsibility for and control of our own destiny that freedom requires. The public's trust in government waxes and wanes. But we have always trusted in ourselves to meet any challenge that required only our ingenuity and industry to surmount. Any "solution" that robs us of that essential sense of ourselves is a cure far worse than the affliction it is meant to treat.

IV. Immigration

Immigration Reform

Letting the People Who Contribute to Society Stay

George W. Bush

President of the United States, 2001– ; born New Haven, CT, July 6, 1946, and raised in Midland and Houston, TX; attended Phillips Academy, Andover, MA; B.A., Yale University, 1968; M.B.A., Harvard Business School, 1975; F-102 pilot, Texas Air National Guard, 1968–73; oil and gas business, Midland, TX, 1975–86; senior adviser in father George H. W. Bush's presidential campaign, 1987–88; one of the partners who purchased the Texas Rangers baseball franchise, 1989, and managing general partner of the team, 1989–94; governor of Texas, 1995–2000.

Editor's introduction: In the spring of 2006, President George W. Bush proposed the most far-reaching immigration reform in decades. As he explains in this address to the nation, which he delivered from the Oval Office, the primary aim of his initiative is strengthening security on the Mexican border. In addition to increasing the number of border patrol agents, he proposes creating a temporary-worker program that would provide legal status to millions of foreign nationals who travel to the United States to work on a temporary basis. "The reality is that there are many people on the other side of our border who will do anything to come to America to work and build a better life," he says. Though in the speech Bush declares his opposition to an amnesty for undocumented immigrants, which he believes "would be unfair to those who are here lawfully," many legislators, particularly in his own party, were skeptical, characterizing aspects of the bill as tantamount to full amnesty. By June 2007 support for the initiative had collapsed in the Senate, and few hold out hope that Bush can revive its prospects in the short time left in his presidency.

George W. Bush's speech: Good evening. I've asked for a few minutes of your time to discuss a matter of national importance—the reform of America's immigration system.

The issue of immigration stirs intense emotions, and in recent weeks, Americans have seen those emotions on display. On the streets of major cities, crowds have rallied in support of those in our country illegally. At our southern border, others have organized to stop illegal immigrants from coming in. Across the country, Americans are trying to reconcile these contrasting images. And in Wash-

Delivered on May 15, 2006, at Washington, D.C.

ington, the debate over immigration reform has reached a time of decision. Tonight, I will make it clear where I stand, and where I want to lead our country on this vital issue.

We must begin by recognizing the problems with our immigration system. For decades, the United States has not been in complete control of its borders. As a result, many who want to work in our economy have been able to sneak across our border, and millions have stayed.

Once here, illegal immigrants live in the shadows of our society. Many use forged documents to get jobs, and that makes it difficult for employers to verify that the workers they hire are legal. Illegal immigration puts pressure on public schools and hospitals, it strains state and local budgets, and brings crime to our communities. These are real problems. Yet we must remember that the vast majority of illegal immigrants are decent people who work hard, support their families, practice their faith, and lead responsible lives. They are a part of American life, but they are beyond the reach and protection of American law.

We're a nation of laws, and we must enforce our laws. We're also a nation of immigrants, and we must uphold that tradition, which has strengthened our country in so many ways. These are not contradictory goals. America can be a lawful society and a welcoming society at the same time. We will fix the problems created by illegal immigration, and we will deliver a system that is secure, orderly, and fair. So I support comprehensive immigration reform that will accomplish five clear objectives.

First, the United States must secure its borders. This is a basic responsibility of a sovereign nation. It is also an urgent requirement of our national security. Our objective is straightforward: The border should be open to trade and lawful immigration, and shut to illegal immigrants, as well as criminals, drug dealers, and terrorists.

I was a governor of a state that has a 1,200-mile border with Mexico. So I know how difficult it is to enforce the border, and how important it is. Since I became President, we've increased funding for border security by 66 percent, and expanded the Border Patrol from about 9,000 to 12,000 agents. The men and women of our Border Patrol are doing a fine job in difficult circumstances, and over the past five years, they have apprehended and sent home about six million people entering America illegally.

Despite this progress, we do not yet have full control of the border, and I am determined to change that. Tonight I'm calling on Congress to provide funding for dramatic improvements in manpower and technology at the border. By the end of 2008, we'll increase the number of Border Patrol officers by an additional 6,000. When these new agents are deployed, we'll have more than doubled the size of the Border Patrol during my presidency.

At the same time, we're launching the most technologically advanced border security initiative in American history. We will construct high-tech fences in urban corridors, and build new patrol roads and barriers in rural areas. We'll employ motion sensors, infrared cameras, and unmanned aerial vehicles to prevent illegal crossings. America has the best technology in the world, and we will ensure that the Border Patrol has the technology they need to do their job and secure our border.

Training thousands of new Border Patrol agents and bringing the most advanced technology to the border will take time. Yet the need to secure our border is urgent. So I'm announcing several immediate steps to strengthen border enforcement during this period of transition:

One way to help during this transition is to use the National Guard. So, in coordination with governors, up to 6,000 Guard members will be deployed to our southern border. The Border Patrol will remain in the lead. The Guard will assist the Border Patrol by operating surveillance systems, analyzing intelligence, installing fences and vehicle barriers, building patrol roads, and providing training. Guard units will not be involved in direct law enforcement activities—that duty will be done by the Border Patrol. This initial commitment of Guard members would last for a period of one year. After that, the number of Guard forces will be reduced as new Border Patrol agents and new technologies come online. It is important for Americans to know that we have enough Guard forces to win the war on terror, to respond to natural disasters, and to help secure our border.

The United States is not going to militarize the southern border. Mexico is our neighbor, and our friend. We will continue to work cooperatively to improve security on both sides of the border, to confront common problems like drug trafficking and crime, and to reduce illegal immigration.

Another way to help during this period of transition is through state and local law enforcement in our border communities. So we'll increase federal funding for state and local authorities assisting the Border Patrol on targeted enforcement missions. We will give state and local authorities the specialized training they need to help federal officers apprehend and detain illegal immigrants. State and local law enforcement officials are an important part of our border security and they need to be a part of our strategy to secure our borders.

The steps I've outlined will improve our ability to catch people entering our country illegally. At the same time, we must ensure that every illegal immigrant we catch crossing our southern border is returned home. More than 85 percent of the illegal immigrants we catch crossing the southern border are Mexicans, and most are sent back home within 24 hours. But when we catch illegal immigrants from other country [sic] it is not as easy to send them home. For many years, the government did not have enough space in our detention facilities to hold them while the legal process unfolded. So most were released back into our society and asked to return for a court date. When the date arrived, the vast majority did not show up. This practice, called "catch and release," is unacceptable, and we will end it.

We're taking several important steps to meet this goal. We've expanded the number of beds in our detention facilities, and we will continue to add more. We've expedited the legal process to cut the average deportation time. And we're making it clear to foreign governments that they must accept back their citizens who violate our immigration laws. As a result of these actions, we've ended "catch and release" for illegal immigrants from some countries. And I will ask Congress for additional funding and legal authority, so we can end "catch and release" at the southern border once and for all. When people know that they'll be caught and sent home if they enter our country illegally, they will be less likely to try to sneak in.

Second, to secure our border, we must create a temporary worker program. The reality is that there are many people on the other side of our border who will do anything to come to America to work and build a better life. They walk across miles of desert in the summer heat, or hide in the back of 18-wheelers to reach our country. This creates enormous pressure on our border that walls and patrols alone will not stop. To secure the border effectively, we must reduce the numbers of people trying to sneak across.

Therefore, I support a temporary worker program that would create a legal path for foreign workers to enter our country in an orderly way, for a limited period of time. This program would match willing foreign workers with willing American employers for jobs Americans are not doing. Every worker who applies for the program would be required to pass criminal background checks. And temporary workers must return to their home country at the conclusion of their stay.

A temporary worker program would meet the needs of our economy, and it would give honest immigrants a way to provide for their families while respecting the law. A temporary worker program would reduce the appeal of human smugglers, and make it less likely that people would risk their lives to cross the border. It would ease the financial burden on state and local governments, by replacing illegal workers with lawful taxpayers. And above all, a temporary worker program would add to our security by making certain we know who is in our country and why they are here.

Third, we need to hold employers to account for the workers they hire. It is against the law to hire someone who is in this country illegally. Yet businesses often cannot verify the legal status of their employees because of the widespread problem of document fraud. Therefore, comprehensive immigration reform must include a better system for verifying documents and work eligibility. A key part of that system should be a new identification card for every legal foreign worker. This card should use biometric technology, such as digital fingerprints, to make it tamper-proof. A tamper-proof card would help us enforce the law, and leave employers with no excuse for violating it. And by making it harder for illegal immigrants to find work in our country, we would discourage people from crossing the border illegally in the first place.

Fourth, we must face the reality that millions of illegal immigrants are here already. They should not be given an automatic path to citizenship. This is amnesty, and I oppose it. Amnesty would be unfair to those who are here lawfully, and it would invite further waves of illegal immigration.

Some in this country argue that the solution is to deport every illegal immigrant, and that any proposal short of this amounts to amnesty. I disagree. It is neither wise, nor realistic to round up millions of people, many with deep roots in the United States, and send them across the border. There is a rational middle ground between granting an automatic path to citizenship for every illegal immigrant, and a program of mass deportation. That middle ground recognizes there are differences between an illegal immigrant who crossed the border recently, and someone who has worked here for many years, and has a home, a family, and an otherwise clean record.

I believe that illegal immigrants who have roots in our country and want to stay should have to pay a meaningful penalty for breaking the law, to pay their taxes, to learn English, and to work in a job for a number of years. People who meet these conditions should be able to apply for citizenship, but approval would not be automatic, and they will have to wait in line behind those who played by the rules and followed the law. What I've just described is not amnesty, it is a way for those who have broken the law to pay their debt to society, and demonstrate the character that makes a good citizen.

Fifth, we must honor the great American tradition of the melting pot, which has made us one nation out of many peoples. The success of our country depends upon helping newcomers assimilate into our society, and embrace our common identity as Americans. Americans are bound together by our shared ideals, an appreciation of our history, respect for the flag we fly, and an ability to speak and write the English language. English is also the key to unlocking the opportunity of America. English allows newcomers to go from picking crops to opening a grocery, from cleaning offices to running offices, from a life of low-paying jobs to a diploma, a career, and a home of their own. When immigrants assimilate and advance in our society, they realize their dreams, they renew our spirit, and they add to the unity of America.

Tonight, I want to speak directly to members of the House and the Senate: An immigration reform bill needs to be comprehensive, because all elements of this problem must be addressed together, or none of them will be solved at all. The House has passed an immigration bill. The Senate should act by the end of this month so we can work out the differences between the two bills, and Congress can pass a comprehensive bill for me to sign into law.

America needs to conduct this debate on immigration in a reasoned and respectful tone. Feelings run deep on this issue, and as we work it out, all of us need to keep some things in mind. We cannot build a unified country by inciting people to anger, or playing on anyone's fears, or exploiting the issue of immigration for political gain. We must always remember that real lives will be affected by our debates and decisions, and that every human being has dignity and value no matter what their citizenship papers say.

I know many of you listening tonight have a parent or a grandparent who came here from another country with dreams of a better life. You know what freedom meant to them, and you know that America is a more hopeful country because of their hard work and sacrifice. As President, I've had the opportunity to meet people of many backgrounds, and hear what America means to them. On a visit to Bethesda Naval Hospital, Laura and I met a wounded Marine named Guadalupe Denogean. Master Gunnery Sergeant Denogean came to the United States from Mexico when he was a boy. He spent his summers picking crops with his family, and then he volunteered for the United States Marine Corps as soon as he was able. During the liberation of Iraq, Master Gunnery Sergeant Denogean was seriously injured. And when asked if he had any requests, he made two: a promotion for the corporal who helped rescue him, and the chance to become an American citizen. And when this brave Marine raised his right hand, and swore an oath to become a citizen of the country he had defended for more than 26 years, I was honored to stand at his side.

We will always be proud to welcome people like Guadalupe Denogean as fellow Americans. Our new immigrants are just what they've always been—people willing to risk everything for the dream of freedom. And America remains what she has always been: the great hope on the horizon, an open door to the future, a blessed and promised land. We honor the heritage of all who come here, no matter where they come from, because we trust in our country's genius for making us all Americans—one nation under God.

Thank you, and good night.

Comprehensive Immigration Reform for a Growing Economy

Carlos M. Gutierrez

U.S. secretary of commerce, 2005– ; born Havana, Cuba, November 4, 1953; sales representative, Kellogg de Mexico, Mexico City, 1975; supervisor of Latin American marketing services, Kellogg Co., Battle Creek, MI, 1982; manager of international marketing services, Kellogg Co., 1983; general manager, Kellogg de Mexico, 1984; president and CEO, Kellogg Canada Inc., 1989; vice president, product development, Kellogg Co., 1990; vice president, sales and marketing, Kellogg USA, 1990; executive vice president, Kellogg USA, 1993; general manager, Kellogg USA Cereal Division, 1993; executive vice president, Kellogg Co., and president, Kellogg Asia-Pacific, 1994; executive vice president, business development, Kellogg Co., 1996; president and COO, Kellogg Co., 1998; elected to corporate board of directors, Kellogg Co., 1998; president and CEO, Kellogg Co., 1999–2004; chairman, Kellogg Co., 2000.

Editor's introduction: When President Bush nominated Carlos M. Gutierrez to be the 35th secretary of the U.S. Department of Commerce, he characterized him as someone who "understands the world of business, from the first rung on the ladder to the very top. He knows exactly what it takes to help American businesses grow and to create jobs." In the following speech, which Gutierrez delivered before the conservative Cato Institute, in Washington, D.C., the secretary argues that immigration is "a key to our future economic health." Noting that many industrialized nations with declining birth rates will increasingly require foreign immigrants to augment their labor force, Gutierrez believes the United States—historically a nation of immigrants—will be at a distinct advantage. An immigrant to the United States from his native Cuba, Gutierrez offers a stirring endorsement of the president's immigration reform bill, declaring, "It is a false choice to think the immigration debate is a battle between America being a welcoming society and being a nation of laws."

Carlos M. Gutierrez's speech: Thank you, Dan. I appreciate the opportunity to speak at the Cato Institute.

The Institute is known for supporting individual liberty and free markets, among other important principles. You also encourage intelligent debate [on] important issues of our day.

I appreciate that, and your efforts to promote a robust and competitive economy.

Delivered on August 1, 2006, at Washington, D.C.

Before I begin, I just want to talk about Cuba since it has been on the news.

At a time of great uncertainty, we want to let the people of Cuba know that we affirm our commitment—when a transition government committed to democracy is in place—we will provide aid, in areas such as food and medicine, economic recovery, and free and fair elections.

The people of Cuba have a choice: economic and political freedom and opportunity, or more political repression and economic suffering under the current regime.

We pledge to help them attain political and economic liberty.

We pledge to extend a hand of friendship and support as they build a democratic government, a strong economy and a brighter tomorrow for their families and their country.

And we pledge to discourage third parties from obstructing the will of the Cuban people.

And let me be very clear: The United States and our citizens pose no threat to the security or the homes of the Cuban people.

President Bush recognizes that Cuba belongs to the Cuban people, and that the future of Cuba is in the hands of Cubans.

And we continue to be concerned about the importance of the Cuban people observing safe, orderly, and legal plans for migration.

Now, let's talk about immigration.

I believe immigration is the domestic social issue of our time—and a key to our future economic health.

America has dealt with difficult immigration issues in the past. There have been large waves of immigrants from Asia, Western Europe, and Eastern Europe, throughout our history.

In fact, proportionately, we have fewer foreign-born people living in the United States today than we did in 1890. In 1890, 14.8 percent of our population was foreign-born. In 2004, 12 percent was foreign born.

So, the challenges of immigration are not new for America, and I believe they create tremendous opportunities.

We are competing in a global economy. Many countries, including Germany, China, and Japan will face declining populations in the future.

All major industrial economies are experiencing substantial growth in their population aged 65 and over. By 2025, the median age of German citizens will increase from 39 to 50 years old. Japan will also see a 46 percent growth in this age group by 2020.

The U.S. will also see our median age growing from 34 to 43. And every 60 seconds, a baby boomer turns 60.

But what separates us from other nations is our ability to assimilate immigrants and incorporate them into our workforce.

From 2000 to 2004, the U.S. Census Bureau estimated that total U.S. population grew by more than 12 million. Forty-four percent of the growth resulted from immigration.

We have an incredible advantage. We can stand out from the pack by using our well-honed skills from 230 years of assimilating immigrants.

But to address the challenges of illegal immigration, take advantage of the opportunities, and strengthen our country for the rest of the century, we must show leadership. We must face reality. We must deal with immigration as it is, not as we wish it were. We must thoughtfully work through the issues, and avoid letting emotion take over the debate.

I am encouraged that we are starting to reach some consensus:

- Recently, more than 500 of our nation's top economists, including five Nobel Laureates, sent a letter to President Bush and all members of Congress. These economists (with diverse political views) stated unequivocally that immigration has been a net gain for American citizens.

- And two-thirds of American voters say they support bills that include a temporary worker program or path to citizenship, rather than one that focuses solely on border security.

President Bush's vision for comprehensive immigration reform:

- Protects our borders—our immigration system can't work if we can't control our borders.

- It recognizes the needs of a growing economy.

Our economy is growing faster than any other large, industrialized nation.

The reality is that we have jobs that American citizens either aren't willing to or aren't available to do.

Our unemployment rate is below the average of the past four decades. I continually hear from industries that they are having difficulty finding workers. We need sources of labor from other countries to fill jobs that aren't getting filled.

The President's proposal upholds our values. We are both a nation of laws and a nation of immigrants.

1. Priority number one in the President's comprehensive proposal is securing our borders.

The President has proposed:

- Increasing the number of Border Patrol agents from 12,000 to 18,000;

- Increasing the amount of technology we have at the borders, so we can know who is coming through;

- And improving processes to become more efficient.

In May, President Bush committed 6,000 National Guard troops to our Southwest border states. This week, we will have 6,000 National Guard members supporting Border Patrol agents along our borders as promised. The Guard's efforts are already making a positive difference. It is also helping that the Department of Homeland Security has stopped the practice of "catch and release," with every population except for one, and instead is using "catch and remove."

- Already the number of captured illegal immigrants has fallen by 45 percent since spring—as fewer crossings are attempted during a normally high-volume season.

- And there's been a 7 percent drop in immigrant deaths in the desert, compared with last year.

- Clearly, the message is out that we have stepped up security at our border.

One of the best ways to secure our borders is to have immigration enforcement inside our country—in the interior.

2. We need effective interior enforcement. That may be the best way to secure our borders.

Our system needs to be fixed.

We have an underground industry built on producing false documentation for illegal workers.

Employers have a hard time helping enforce the law because they are not sure what documents they should require.

- A Government Accountability Office report last year found that document fraud and the large number of documents acceptable for proving work eligibility have caused significant confusion among employers.

The rules must be clear enough to hold businesses accountable for hiring people with the proper documentation. With comprehensive reform, we will ensure that businesses have the tools they need to do this, and that we can hold them accountable.

That's why we need a temporary worker's program. It would create a legal means for workers to enter the United States for a limited time.

And we need a biometric card identification system. We have the technology today to quickly and effectively use a person's unique characteristics, such as a fingerprint, to verify immigration status.

When we have a biometric system—and we have a temporary worker's program—dynamics will change.

Over time, it will become unlikely that people will risk their lives coming across the border illegally if it is well-known that unless you have the temporary worker's permit, you will not find a job.

This is one of the most consequential things we can do to make our borders more secure. And it demonstrates the wisdom of comprehensive immigration reform.

3. The other reality we must confront is that we have 12 million people who are in the country illegally. This issue will not be resolved by ignoring it, or waiting longer to confront it.

Think about the task of deporting 12 millions individuals. Is that something we are going to do as a country? The President has said it wouldn't be wise, practical, or humane.

It would require separating parents from their 3 million American-born children. Some say the children could decide if they go with their parents or stay. Can you imagine that?

Mass deportation is an extreme position, and it's not realistic.

The other extreme is amnesty. The dictionary defines amnesty as an "unconditional pardon—obliterating all memory of the offense." The President does not support amnesty, and it's not accurate or fair to call his solution amnesty.

We're talking about having a hard-earned path to legalization, which would require meeting conditions:

- People waiting their turn in line,

- Paying fines,

- Paying taxes,

- Learning English,

- Undergoing a criminal background check,

- And having a job.

Some argue that we are simply repeating the mistakes of the Immigration Reform and Control Act, which passed Congress in 1986. I want to make it perfectly clear that the President's proposal addresses the shortcomings of the 1986 law.

The 1986 law missed the importance of strengthening border security. The President has deployed the National Guard and is doubling the number of Border Patrol agents.

The 1986 law didn't address what draws illegal immigrants to cross our borders: that people are coming here to work. It didn't provide a Temporary Workers Program to allow those who want to work and return to do so. And it did not provide a legal means to address the needs of American businesses.

Today, we have technology that was not available in 1986. With biometric cards and the Basic Pilot system, we can hold employers accountable to verify their workers' status.

The 1986 law was not followed by any real enforcement. In contrast, the President is calling for more criminal sanctions, instead of just administrative fines.

And the 1986 law provided amnesty for 3 million illegal immigrants. As I said, the President opposes amnesty, and believes people must earn any legalization.

Earlier this month, 33 conservative leaders wrote, "The best way—the only way—to realize President Reagan's vision is through comprehensive immigration reform legislation."

The issues of illegal immigration are far too complex to presume they can be solved with one easy action.

What we need is leadership and reasonable compromise in the middle. We need to be talking about the right mix of immigration reform that addresses all the issues—and acknowledges that extremes aren't viable.

Just last week, Senator Kay Bailey Hutchison and Representative Mike Pence offered an intriguing proposal. It provides for strong border security, while also recognizing our economy's need for temporary workers.

Their proposal acknowledges that we must secure our borders to secure our nation. The President has already taken bold steps in this direction.

Obviously, there are many details to be worked out. I met with Senator Hutchison and Congressman Pence, and they both believe their proposal is a starting point. We encourage the House and Senate to continue talking, and to continue this rational approach to finding solutions.

4. The other important point that President Bush makes is that we are a nation of immigrants.

And immigrants have helped make this country great. All of us here today—unless you are Native American—are immigrants or descendants of immigrants.

I'll give you my personal perspective: I came to this country in 1960 from Cuba. I was a six-year-old immigrant. On January 4, 1966, I formally became a U.S. citizen. To this day, my U.S. passport is my most valued material possession.

I'm extremely grateful that people encouraged—even pushed me—to learn the language and assimilate.

I'm also very thankful for the opportunities this country has given me. I believe that immigrants today just want an opportunity.

It is a false choice to think the immigration debate is a battle between America being a welcoming society and being a nation of laws.

We can be both because we are both. I ask you to commit yourself to comprehensive immigration reform. We all need to contribute to the solution.

Comprehensive immigration reform will make our country stronger, and I'm convinced that future generations will be proud of what we did. Thank you, and God bless you.

And now, I'll be glad to take your questions.

Immigration Bill Hurts Workers

Bernie Sanders

*U.S. senator (I), Vermont 2007– ; born Brooklyn, NY, September 8, 1941;
B.A., University of Chicago, 1964; freelance writer, carpenter, youth counse-
lor, 1964–76; director, American People's Historical Society, Burlington,
VT, 1976–81; mayor, Burlington, VT, 1981–89; faculty, Harvard University, 1989; faculty, Hamilton College, Clinton, NY, 1990; U.S. representative (I), Vermont, 1991–2007; U.S. Senate committees: Budget; Veterans;
Energy; Environment; and Health, Education, Labor, and Pensions.*

Editor's introduction: This summer, after the Senate voted 53–46
to set aside the president's immigration reform legislation, Senator
Bernie Sanders said, "At a time when the middle class is shrinking,
poverty is increasing and millions of Americans are working longer
hours for lower wages it makes no sense to me to have an immigration bill which, over a period of years, would bring millions of 'guest
workers' into this country who are prepared to work for lower wages
than American workers. We need to increase wages in this country,
not lower them." Shortly before, on June 20, at a Capitol Hill news
conference—in which Sanders was joined by AFL-CIO Secretary-
Treasurer Richard L. Trumka; Ed Sullivan, president of the Building and Construction Trades Department of the AFL-CIO; and
United Food and Commercial Workers President Joe Hansen—the
senator delivered the following speech, which outlines his concerns
over how immigration reform could affect American workers.

Bernie Sanders's speech: There has been, needless to say, a lot of
debate about the Senate immigration bill. Unfortunately, almost all
of that debate has centered on illegal immigration and has
down-played the very consequential provisions in this bill dealing
with "guest workers."

Let's be very clear about what's happening economically in America today. While the wealthiest people have never had it so good, the
middle class is shrinking, poverty is increasing, and millions of
Americans are working longer hours for lower wages.

Since President Bush has been in office, median income for work-
ing-age families has declined each and every year. Ominously, even
college graduates are now beginning to see a decline in real earnings. And, the American people understand very clearly what is
going on economically. A recent Gallup Poll showed that almost 70
percent of Americans believe that the economy is getting worse.

Delivered on June 20, 2007, at Washington, D.C.

And, another recent poll showed that by nearly a two-to-one margin, Americans believe that life for the middle class has gotten worse over the past decade.

In the midst of this harsh and tragic economic reality, we need legislation which will improve wages and income in America, lower the poverty rate and expand the middle class.

Unfortunately, the guest worker provisions in this bill will only make a bad situation even worse, will drive down wages even further, not only for low-wage workers, but for highly-skilled professionals as well.

The same corporations that supported disastrous trade agreements such as NAFTA and PNTR with China (which have cost us millions of good-paying jobs), the same anti-worker businesses that have fought against an increase in the minimum wage, and that vigorously oppose the rights of workers to unionize, the same business groups that have proudly proclaimed their belief in outsourcing, and have literally urged companies to move American jobs abroad, are many of the same exact companies who are strongly supporting this bill and the guest worker programs contained in it.

> What companies that employ both low-wage and high-skill employees want is to defy the economic law of supply and demand.

Why? The answer is simple. What companies that employ both low-wage and high-skill employees want is to defy the economic law of supply and demand.

Instead of paying American workers higher wages and better benefits if there are labor shortages, their solution is to simply bring low-wage workers in from abroad. And let me tell you, there is a never-ending supply of low-wage workers from all over the world who would be delighted to work in America.

In terms of guest worker programs for low-wage workers, corporate America claims it needs foreign workers to do the jobs "that Americans just won't do."

Really? If these same companies raised wages and provided decent benefits for their workers instead of lowering wages and benefits, I think they would find more than enough Americans flocking to those jobs. In fact, Wal-Mart, which is part of one of the coalitions supporting this immigration bill, found that thousands of workers applied for a few hundred of their jobs at two of their stores that they recently opened—even though their wages are not particularly good.

And, in terms of professional jobs, the corporate supporters of this legislation tell us they need more H-1B visas because Americans presumably aren't smart enough to be computer professionals, engineers, university professors, accountants, financial analysts, nurses, psychologists, lawyers, elementary school teachers, etc., etc.

Well, I certainly don't believe that.

Finally, on top of everything else, while high-tech companies like IBM, Motorola and Dell are telling Congress that they need to import more high-skilled workers from overseas, these very same companies are busy laying-off thousands of American workers.

It is absolutely clear that our current immigration policies are a mess and we need to make changes. In my view, however, we must and can do that in a way that does not further undermine the working families of our country who are already under severe economic duress.

Threats to U.S. National Security

Deportation Policies that Force Families Apart

Charles B. Rangel

U.S. representative (D), New York's 15th District, 1971– ; born New York City, June 11, 1930; B.S., New York University, 1957; J.D., St. John's University, 1960; admitted to the Bar of New York State, 1960; private law practice, New York City, 1960–61; assistant U.S. attorney for the Southern District of New York, 1961–62; served as legal counsel to various organizations and officials, 1963–66; state representative, New York's 72nd District, New York State Assembly, 1966–70; founding member, Congressional Black Caucus, 1974– ; congressional committees: Ways and Means (chairman).

Editor's introduction: As the U.S. representative for the 15th Congressional district, located in New York City, Charles Rangel has long served as an advocate for immigrants. This is perhaps not surprising, given that his home state has the second highest percentage of foreign-born residents in the nation after California, and his hometown is one of the few cities in the world with over a million foreign-born residents. When hundreds of thousands of Americans mobilized on May 1, 2007, to march in opposition to some of the reforms proposed by the Bush administration, Rangel offered them his support, saying, "This fight is far from over. We have to continue to build coalitions and get everyone—citizens, immigrants and native-born Americans—to come out and say 'No, we don't have to choose between security and fairness. Yes, we can have an immigration policy that keeps this land safe without turning our backs on our immigrant past.'" In the following speech, which he delivered on the floor of Congress, Rangel draws attention to the ramifications of certain U.S. deportation policies and calls for their reform.

Charles B. Rangel's speech: Madam Speaker, conversations on this very important topic are necessary to recognize the consequences of criminally convicted U.S. residents deported to Latin America and the Caribbean. I commend Chairman *Engel* for taking an interest and exploring the challenges that our deportation policies have imposed on the region. I look forward to working with you and the Committee, as you examine this issue.

Recently, the Presidents and Prime Ministers of the Caribbean Community (CARICOM) visited the U.S. Congress. They spoke with several members and met with committees regarding the issues affecting the region. One major concern for them is the impact of

---

Delivered on July 27, 2007, at Washington, D.C.

thousands of criminally convicted deportees from the United States to the nations of the Caribbean. At times these individuals are repatriated without notice to the receiving country, regardless of the impact their arrival will have upon the societies to which they are being sent. The adverse impact of this practice is not only felt in the Caribbean, but in our communities as well, due to the financial burden it places on the families left behind without means of support.

The CARICOM members are not asking for a change in the policy, but adjustment to how it is executed. The CARICOM members understand that residence permits are a privilege granted to non-citizens contingent on their good behavior. Clearly, the commission of a crime does not constitute good behavior. However, mothers and fathers are being separated from their families without making the appropriate provisions for the welfare of children who remain in our country. Those repatriated sometimes have no support units in their country of citizenship and are forced into a life of poverty, as well as stigmatized for being deported. In addition, the families they leave behind are left with huge legal bills or in situations where they have to fend off poverty. It is my contention that poverty is a threat to the national security of the United States.

> We need to support initiatives to integrate repatriated individuals into their new society.

The Human Rights Watch in their July 2007 Report entitled "Forced Apart Families Separated and Immigrants Harmed by United States Deportation Policy" stated that since 1996 approximately 1.6 million families have been torn apart by the U.S. deportation policies. The top ten countries of origin for non-citizens removed on criminal grounds represent Latin America and the Caribbean, Mexico being the most affected of these nations, with over 500,000 Mexican nationals being repatriated between FY 1997 and FY 2005. Haiti, the poorest nation in our hemisphere, is among the top ten with over 3,000 individuals being returned to that nation. Many parents explained that their children, the vast majority of whom had been left in the deporting country, faced extreme hardships, both emotionally and financially. These are American children that are forced into situations where they have to abandon school to support their families. These are American children sometimes forced to live in single-parent households or households without a parent, ushered into a life of poverty. Poverty not only pricks our conscience, but it short changes our future as well. Society ultimately pays for poverty through a less productive workforce, more crime, higher use of welfare, greater drug addiction and other social ills.

We need to support initiatives to integrate repatriated individuals into their new society. Often they have spent their entire life in the United States and lack a support system in the receiving country. Recommendations that need to be explored include funding to expand or establish resettlement programs. These programs should be geared to setting up transition centers where individuals are afforded basic resources such as food, clothing and shelter. Job training programs and social service type institutions need to be reinforced in the region, since upon deportation, many of them drift into homelessness, and with no job prospects, they end up doing crime as a means of survival.

There needs to be the creation of a system to track and monitor high-risk criminal deportees. In some situations criminals are repatriated and no formal processing takes place in the receiving country. In essence they are let loose into the community and there are no systems in place to track their movement in the receiving country. It is believed that there is a correlation between the increase in gang related activity in the region and deportees. These individuals often make their way back into the U.S. or form part of trans-national organized crime units.

I am glad to see that this hearing has been convened to explore ways this Congress can help our neighbors in the region address this issue. Failing to properly reintegrate repatriated individuals is a challenge that negatively impacts our neighbors and threatens our national security.

V. Global Climate Change

Global Warming Is an Immediate Crisis

Al Gore

Co-founder and chairman, Generation Investment Management LLC, 2004– ; co-founder and chairman, Current TV satellite television network, 2004– ; Born Washington, D.C., March 31, 1948; B.A. Harvard University, 1969; U.S. Army, 1969–1971; reporter, The Tennessean, 1971–76; home builder and land developer, Tanglewood Home Builders Co., 1971–76; student, Graduate School of Religion, Vanderbilt University, 1971–72; student, Vanderbilt University Law School, 1974–76; U.S. representative (D), Tennesse's Fourth District; U.S. senator (D), Tennessee, 1985–93; vice president of the United States, 1993–2001; visiting professor, Columbia University Graduate School of Journalism, Fisk University, University of California at Los Angeles, Middle Tennessee State University; Nobel Peace Prize recipient, 2007; author: Earth in the Balance: Ecology and the Human Spirit *(1992);* The Assault on Reason *(2004);* An Inconvenient Truth *(2006).*

Editor's introduction: Since narrowly losing the highly disputed 2000 presidential election, former vice president Al Gore has earned widespread acclaim for his speeches on environmental issues, particularly global warming. *An Inconvenient Truth*, a documentary film chronicling Gore's efforts to educate the public about the global climate crisis, was a surprise hit at the box office and won the Academy Award for best documentary in 2007. The companion book was also a *New York Times* bestseller. Moreover, in October 2007, Gore's efforts to raise public awareness earned him a Nobel Peace Prize. In this speech, delivered at the New York University School of Law, Gore outlines what he believes to be a "responsible approach to the climate crisis."

Al Gore's speech: Ladies and Gentlemen:

Thank you Paul and Jim for those kind introductions. I would especially like to thank our host, New York University and the President of the College John Sexton and the Dean of the Law School Richard Revesz. I am also grateful to our co-sponsors, the World Resources Institute and Set America Free.

A few days ago, scientists announced alarming new evidence of the rapid melting of the perennial ice of the north polar cap, continuing a trend of the past several years that now confronts us with the prospect that human activities, if unchecked in the next decade, could destroy one of the earth's principal mechanisms for cooling itself. Another group of scientists presented evidence that human

---

Delivered on September 18, 2006, at New York, NY. Reprinted with permission.

activities are responsible for the dramatic warming of sea surface temperatures in the areas of the ocean where hurricanes form. A few weeks earlier, new information from yet another team showed dramatic increases in the burning of forests throughout the American West, a trend that has increased decade by decade, as warmer temperatures have dried out soils and vegetation. All these findings come at the end of a summer with record breaking temperatures and the hottest twelve month period ever measured in the U.S., with persistent drought in vast areas of our country. *Scientific American* introduces the lead article in its special issue this month with the following sentence: "The debate on global warming is over."

Many scientists are now warning that we are moving closer to several "tipping points" that could—within as little as 10 years—make it impossible for us to avoid irretrievable damage to the planet's habitability for human civilization. In this regard, just a few weeks ago, another group of scientists reported on the unexpectedly rapid increases in the release of carbon and methane emissions from frozen tundra in Siberia, now beginning to thaw because of human caused increases in global temperature. The scientists tell us that the tundra in danger of thawing contains an amount of additional global warming pollution that is equal to the total amount that is already in the earth's atmosphere. Similarly, earlier this year, yet another team of scientists reported that the previous twelve months saw 32 glacial earthquakes on Greenland between 4.6 and 5.1 on the Richter scale—a disturbing sign that a massive destabilization may now be underway deep within the second largest accumulation of ice on the planet, enough ice to raise sea level 20 feet worldwide if it broke up and slipped into the sea. Each passing day brings yet more evidence that we are now facing a planetary emergency—a climate crisis that demands immediate action to sharply reduce carbon dioxide emissions worldwide in order to turn down the earth's thermostat and avert catastrophe.

The serious debate over the climate crisis has now moved on to the question of how we can craft emergency solutions in order to avoid this catastrophic damage.

This debate over solutions has been slow to start in earnest not only because some of our leaders still find it more convenient to deny the reality of the crisis, but also because the hard truth for the rest of us is that the maximum that seems politically feasible still falls far short of the minimum that would be effective in solving the crisis. This no-man's land—or no politician zone—falling between the farthest reaches of political feasibility and the first beginnings of truly effective change is the area that I would like to explore in my speech today.

T. S. Eliot once wrote: Between the idea and the reality, between the motion and the act falls the shadow. . . . Between the conception and the creation, Between the emotion and the response Falls the Shadow.

My purpose is not to present a comprehensive and detailed blue-print—for that is a task for our democracy as a whole—but rather to try to shine some light on a pathway through this terra incognita that lies between where we are and where we need to go. Because, if we acknowledge candidly that what we need to do is beyond the lim-its of our current political capacities, that really is just another way of saying that we have to urgently expand the limits of what is polit-ically possible.

I have no doubt that we can do precisely that, because having served almost three decades in elected office, I believe I know one thing about America's political system that some of the pessimists do not: it shares something in common with the climate system; it can appear to move only at a slow pace, but it can also cross a tip-ping point beyond which it can move with lightning speed. Just as a single tumbling rock can trigger a massive landslide, America has sometimes experienced sudden avalanches of political change that had their beginnings with what first seemed like small changes.

Two weeks ago, Democrats and Republicans joined together in our largest state, California, to pass legally binding sharp reductions in CO_2 emissions. 295 American cities have now independently "rati-fied" and embraced CO_2 reductions called for in the Kyoto Treaty. 85 conservative evangelical ministers publicly broke with the Bush-Cheney administration to call for bold action to solve the climate cri-sis. Business leaders in both political parties have taken significant steps to position their companies as leaders in this struggle and have adopted a policy that not only reduces CO_2 but makes their companies zero carbon companies. Many of them have discovered a way to increase profits and productivity by eliminating their contri-butions to global warming pollution.

Many Americans are now seeing a bright light shining from the far side of this no-man's land that illuminates not sacrifice and dan-ger, but instead a vision of a bright future that is better for our country in every way—a future with better jobs, a cleaner environ-ment, a more secure nation, and a safer world.

After all, many Americans are tired of borrowing huge amounts of money from China to buy huge amounts of oil from the Persian Gulf to make huge amounts of pollution that destroys the planet's cli-mate. Increasingly, Americans believe that we have to change every part of that pattern.

When I visit port cities like Seattle, New Orleans, or Baltimore, I find massive ships, running low in the water, heavily burdened with foreign cargo or foreign oil arriving by the thousands. These same cargo ships and tankers depart riding high with only ballast water to keep them from rolling over.

One-way trade is destructive to our economic future. We send money, electronically, in the opposite direction. But, we can change this by inventing and manufacturing new solutions to stop global warming right here in America. I still believe in good old-fashioned

American ingenuity. We need to fill those ships with new products and technologies that we create to turn down the global thermostat. Working together, we can create jobs and stop global warming. But we must begin by winning the first key battle—against inertia and the fear of change.

In order to conquer our fear and walk boldly forward on the path that lies before us, we have to insist on a higher level of honesty in America's political dialogue. When we make big mistakes in America, it is usually because the people have not been given an honest accounting of the choices before us. It also is often because too many members of both parties who knew better did not have the courage to do better.

Our children have a right to hold us to a higher standard when their future—indeed the future of all human civilization—is hanging in the balance. They deserve better than the spectacle of censorship of the best scientific evidence about the truth of our situation and harassment of honest scientists who are trying to warn us about the looming catastrophe. They deserve better than politicians who sit on their hands and do nothing to confront the greatest challenge that humankind has ever faced—even as the danger bears down on us.

> In order for the world to respond urgently to the climate crisis, the United States must lead the way.

We in the United States of America have a particularly important responsibility, after all, because the world still regards us—in spite of our recent moral lapses—as the natural leader of the community of nations. Simply put, in order for the world to respond urgently to the climate crisis, the United States must lead the way. No other nation can.

Developing countries like China and India have gained their own understanding of how threatening the climate crisis is to them, but they will never find the political will to make the necessary changes in their growing economies unless and until the United States leads the way. Our natural role is to be the pace car in the race to stop global warming.

So, what would a responsible approach to the climate crisis look like if we had one in America?

Well, first of all, we should start by immediately freezing CO_2 emissions and then beginning sharp reductions. Merely engaging in high-minded debates about theoretical future reductions while continuing to steadily increase emissions represents a self-delusional and reckless approach. In some ways, that approach is worse than doing nothing at all, because it lulls the gullible into thinking that something is actually being done when in fact it is not.

An immediate freeze has the virtue of being clear, simple, and easy to understand. It can attract support across partisan lines as a logical starting point for the more difficult work that lies ahead. I remember a quarter century ago when I was the author of a complex nuclear arms control plan to deal with the then–rampant arms race between our country and the former Soviet Union. At the time, I was strongly opposed to the nuclear freeze movement, which I saw as simplistic and naive. But, ¾ of the American people supported it—and as I look back on those years I see more clearly now that the outpouring of public support for that very simple and clear mandate changed the political landscape and made it possible for more detailed and sophisticated proposals to eventually be adopted.

When the politicians are paralyzed in the face of a great threat, our nation needs a popular movement, a rallying cry, a standard, a mandate that is broadly supported on a bipartisan basis.

A responsible approach to solving this crisis would also involve joining the rest of the global economy in playing by the rules of the world treaty that reduces global warming pollution by authorizing the trading of emissions within a global cap.

At present, the global system for carbon emissions trading is embodied in the Kyoto Treaty. It drives reductions in CO_2 and helps many countries that are a part of the treaty to find the most efficient ways to meet their targets for reductions. It is true that not all countries are yet on track to meet their targets, but the first targets don't have to be met until 2008 and the largest and most important reductions typically take longer than the near term in any case.

The absence of the United States from the treaty means that 25% of the world economy is now missing. It is like filling a bucket with a large hole in the bottom. When the United States eventually joins the rest of the world community in making this system operate well, the global market for carbon emissions will become a highly efficient closed system and every corporate board of directors on earth will have a fiduciary duty to manage and reduce CO_2 emissions in order to protect shareholder value.

Many American businesses that operate in other countries already have to abide by the Kyoto Treaty anyway, and unsurprisingly, they are the companies that have been most eager to adopt these new principles here at home as well. The United States and Australia are the only two countries in the developed world that have not yet ratified the Kyoto Treaty. Since the Treaty has been so demonized in America's internal debate, it is difficult to imagine the current Senate finding a way to ratify it. But the United States should immediately join the discussion that is now underway on the new tougher treaty that will soon be completed. We should plan to accelerate its adoption and phase it in more quickly than is presently planned.

Third, a responsible approach to solutions would avoid the mistake of trying to find a single magic "silver bullet" and recognize that the answer will involve what Bill McKibben has called "silver-buckshot"—numerous important solutions, all of which are hard, but no one of which is by itself the full answer for our problem.

One of the most productive approaches to the "multiple solutions" needed is a road-map designed by two Princeton professors, Rob Socolow and Steven Pacala, which breaks down the overall problem into more manageable parts. Socolow and Pacala have identified 15 or 20 building blocks (or "wedges") that can be used to solve our problem effectively—even if we only use 7 or 8 of them. I am among the many who have found this approach useful as a way to structure a discussion of the choices before us.

Over the next year, I intend to convene an ongoing broad-based discussion of solutions that will involve leaders from government, science, business, labor, agriculture, grass-roots activists, faith communities and others.

I am convinced that it is possible to build an effective consensus in the United States and in the world at large on the most effective approaches to solve the climate crisis. Many of those solutions will be found in the building blocks that currently structure so many discussions. But I am also certain that some of the most powerful solutions will lie beyond our current categories of building blocks and "wedges." Our secret strength in America has always been our capacity for vision. "Make no little plans," one of our most famous architects said over a century ago, "they have no magic to stir men's blood."

I look forward to the deep discussion and debate that lies ahead. But there are already some solutions that seem to stand out as particularly promising:

First, dramatic improvements in the efficiency with which we generate, transport and use energy will almost certainly prove to be the single biggest source of sharp reductions in global warming pollution. Because pollution has been systematically ignored in the old rules of America's marketplace, there are lots of relatively easy ways to use new and more efficient options to cheaply eliminate it. Since pollution is, after all, waste, business and industry usually become more productive and efficient when they systematically go about reducing pollution. After all, many of the technologies on which we depend are actually so old that they are inherently far less efficient than newer technologies that we haven't started using. One of the best examples is the internal combustion engine. When scientists calculate the energy content in BTUs of each gallon of gasoline used in a typical car, and then measure the amounts wasted in the car's routine operation, they find that an incredible 90% of that energy is completely wasted. One engineer, Amory Lovins, has gone farther and calculated the amount of energy that is actually used to move the passenger (excluding the amount of energy used to move the several tons of metal surrounding the passenger) and has found that only 1% of the energy is actually used to move the person. This is more than an arcane calculation, or a parlor trick with arithmetic. These numbers actually illuminate the single biggest opportunity to make our economy more efficient and competitive while sharply reducing global warming pollution.

To take another example, many older factories use obsolete processes that generate prodigious amounts of waste heat that actually has tremendous economic value. By redesigning their processes and capturing all of that waste, they can eliminate huge amounts of global warming pollution while saving billions of dollars at the same time.

When we introduce the right incentives for eliminating pollution and becoming more efficient, many businesses will begin to make greater use of computers and advanced monitoring systems to identify even more opportunities for savings. This is what happened in the computer chip industry when more powerful chips led to better computers, which in turn made it possible to design even more powerful chips, in a virtuous cycle of steady improvement that became known as "Moore's Law." We may well see the emergence of a new version of "Moore's Law" producing steadily higher levels of energy efficiency at steadily lower cost.

There is yet another lesson we can learn from America's success in the information revolution. When the Internet was invented—and I assure you I intend to choose my words carefully here—it was because defense planners in the Pentagon forty years ago were searching for a way to protect America's command and communication infrastructure from being disrupted in a nuclear attack. The network they created—known as ARPANET—was based on "distributed communication" that allowed it to continue functioning even if part of it was destroyed.

> Our nation faces threats very different from those we countered during the Cold War.

Today, our nation faces threats very different from those we countered during the Cold War. We worry today that terrorists might try to inflict great damage on America's energy infrastructure by attacking a single vulnerable part of the oil distribution or electricity distribution network. So, taking a page from the early pioneers of ARPANET, we should develop a distributed electricity and liquid that is less dependent on large coal-fired generating plants and vulnerable oil ports and refineries.

Small windmills and photovoltaic solar cells distributed widely throughout the electricity grid would sharply reduce CO_2 emissions and at the same time increase our energy security. Likewise, widely dispersed ethanol and biodiesel production facilities would shift our transportation fuel stocks to renewable forms of energy while making us less dependent on and vulnerable to disruptions in the supply of expensive crude oil from the Persian Gulf, Venezuela and Nigeria, all of which are extremely unreliable sources upon which to base our future economic vitality. It would also make us less vulnerable to the impact of a category 5 hurricane hitting coastal refineries or to a terrorist attack on ports or key parts of our current energy infrastructure.

Just as a robust information economy was triggered by the intro-duction of the Internet, a dynamic new renewable energy economy can be stimulated by the development of an "electranet," or smart grid, that allows individual homeowners and business-owners any-where in America to use their own renewable sources of energy to sell electricity into the grid when they have a surplus and purchase it from the grid when they don't. The same electranet could give homeowners and business-owners accurate and powerful tools with which to precisely measure how much energy they are using where and when, and identify opportunities for eliminating unnecessary costs and wasteful usage patterns.

A second group of building blocks to solve the climate crisis involves America's transportation infrastructure. We could further increase the value and efficiency of a distributed energy network by retooling our failing auto giants—GM and Ford—to require and assist them in switching to the manufacture of flex-fuel, plug-in, hybrid vehicles. The owners of such vehicles would have the ability to use electricity as a principle source of power and to supplement it by switching from gasoline to ethanol or biodiesel. This flexibility would give them incredible power in the marketplace for energy to push the entire system to much higher levels of efficiency and in the process sharply reduce global warming pollution.

This shift would also offer the hope of saving tens of thousands of good jobs in American companies that are presently fighting a los-ing battle selling cars and trucks that are less efficient than the ones made by their competitors in countries where they were forced to reduce their pollution and thus become more efficient.

It is, in other words, time for a national oil change. That is appar-ent to anyone who has looked at our national dipstick.

Our current ridiculous dependence on oil endangers not only our national security, but also our economic security. Anyone who believes that the international market for oil is a "free market" is seriously deluded. It has many characteristics of a free market, but it is also subject to periodic manipulation by the small group of nations controlling the largest recoverable reserves, sometimes in concert with companies that have great influence over the global production, refining, and distribution network.

It is extremely important for us to be clear among ourselves that these periodic efforts to manipulate price and supply have not one but two objectives. They naturally seek to maximize profits. But even more significantly, they seek to manipulate our political will. Every time we come close to recognizing the wisdom of developing our own independent sources of renewable fuels, they seek to dissi-pate our sense of urgency and derail our effort to become less depen-dent. That is what is happening at this very moment.

Shifting to a greater reliance on ethanol, cellulosic ethanol, butanol, and green diesel fuels will not only reduce global warming pollution and enhance our national and economic security, it will also reverse the steady loss of jobs and income in rural America.

Several important building blocks for America's role in solving the climate crisis can be found in new approaches to agriculture. As pointed out by the "25 by 25" movement (aimed at securing 25% of America's power and transportation fuels from agricultural sources by the year 2025) we can revitalize the farm economy by shifting its mission from a focus on food, feed and fiber to a focus on food, feed, fiber, fuel, and ecosystem services. We can restore the health of depleted soils by encouraging and rewarding the growing of fuel source crops like switchgrass and saw-grass, using no till cultivation, and scientific crop rotation. We should also reward farmers for planting more trees and sequestering more carbon, and recognize the economic value of their stewardship of resources that are important to the health of our ecosystems.

Similarly, we should take bold steps to stop deforestation and extend the harvest cycle on timber to optimize the carbon sequestration that is most powerful and most efficient with older trees. On a worldwide basis, 2 and ½ trillion tons of the 10 trillion tons of CO_2 emitted each year come from burning forests. So, better management of forests is one of the single most important strategies for solving the climate crisis.

Biomass—whether in the form of trees, switchgrass, or other sources—is one of the most important forms of renewable energy. And renewable sources make up one of the most promising building blocks for reducing carbon pollution.

Wind energy is already fully competitive as a mainstream source of electricity and will continue to grow in prominence and profitability.

Solar photovoltaic energy is—according to researchers—much closer than it has ever been to a cost competitive breakthrough, as new nanotechnologies are being applied to dramatically enhance the efficiency with which solar cells produce electricity from sunlight— and as clever new designs for concentrating solar energy are used with new approaches such as Stirling engines that can bring costs sharply down.

Buildings—both commercial and residential—represent a larger source of global warming pollution than cars and trucks. But new architecture and design techniques are creating dramatic new opportunities for huge savings in energy use and global warming pollution. As an example of their potential, the American Institute of Architecture and the National Conference of Mayors have endorsed the "2030 Challenge," asking the global architecture and building community to immediately transform building design to require that all new buildings and developments be designed to use one half the fossil fuel energy they would typically consume for each building type, and that all new buildings be carbon neutral by 2030, using zero fossil fuels to operate. A newly constructed building at

Oberlin College is producing 30 percent energy than it consumes. Some other countries have actually required a standard calling for zero carbon based energy inputs for new buildings.

The rapid urbanization of the world's population is leading to the prospective development of more new urban buildings in the next 35 years than have been constructed in all previous human history. This startling trend represents a tremendous opportunity for sharp reductions in global warming pollution through the use of intelligent architecture and design and stringent standards.

Here in the US the extra cost of efficiency improvements such as thicker insulation and more efficient window coatings have traditionally been shunned by builders and homebuyers alike because they add to the initial purchase price—even though these investments typically pay for themselves by reducing heating and cooling costs and then produce additional savings each month for the lifetime of the building. It should be possible to remove the purchase price barrier for such improvements through the use of innovative mortgage finance instruments that eliminate any additional increase in the purchase price by capturing the future income from the expected savings. We should create a Carbon Neutral Mortgage Association to market these new financial instruments and stimulate their use in the private sector by utilities, banks and homebuilders. This new "Connie Mae" (CNMA) could be a valuable instrument for reducing the pollution from new buildings.

Many believe that a responsible approach to sharply reducing global warming pollution would involve a significant increase in the use of nuclear power plants as a substitute for coal-fired generators. While I am not opposed to nuclear power and expect to see some modest increased use of nuclear reactors, I doubt that they will play a significant role in most countries as a new source of electricity. The main reason for my skepticism about nuclear power playing a much larger role in the world's energy future is not the problem of waste disposal or the danger of reactor operator error, or the vulnerability to terrorist attack. Let's assume for the moment that all three of these problems can be solved. That still leaves two serious issues that are more difficult constraints. The first is economics; the current generation of reactors is expensive, take a long time to build, and only come in one size—extra large. In a time of great uncertainty over energy prices, utilities must count on great uncertainty in electricity demand—and that uncertainty causes them to strongly prefer smaller incremental additions to their generating capacity that are each less expensive and quicker to build than are large 1000 megawatt light water reactors. Newer, more scalable and affordable reactor designs may eventually become available, but not soon. Secondly, if the world as a whole chose nuclear power as the option of choice to replace coal-fired generating plants, we would face a dramatic increase in the likelihood of nuclear weapons proliferation. During my 8 years in the White House, every nuclear weapons proliferation issue we dealt with was connected to a nuclear reactor program. Today, the dangerous weapons programs in both Iran and North Korea are linked to their civilian reactor programs. Moreover, proposals to separate the ownership of reactors from the ownership of the fuel supply process have met with stiff resistance from developing countries who want reactors. As a result of all these problems, I believe that nuclear reactors will only play a limited role.

The most important set of problems that must be solved in charting solutions for the climate crisis have to do with coal, one of the dirtiest sources of energy that produces far more CO_2 for each unit of energy output than oil or gas. Yet, coal is found in abundance in the United States, China, and many other places. Because the pollution from the burning of coal is currently excluded from the market calculations of what it costs, coal is presently the cheapest source of abundant energy. And its relative role is growing rapidly day by day.

Fortunately, there may be a way to capture the CO_2 produced as coal as burned and sequester it safely to prevent it from adding to the climate crisis. It is not easy. This technique, known as carbon capture and sequestration (CCS) is expensive and most users of coal have resisted the investments necessary to use it. However, when the cost of *not* using it is calculated, it becomes obvious that CCS will play a significant and growing role as one of the major building blocks of a solution to the climate crisis.

Interestingly, the most advanced and environmentally responsible project for capturing and sequestering CO_2 is in one of the most forbidding locations for energy production anywhere in the world—in the Norwegian portions of the North Sea. Norway, as it turns out, has hefty CO_2 taxes; and, even though there are many exceptions and exemptions, oil production is not one of them. As a result, the oil producers have found it quite economical and profitable to develop and use advanced CCS technologies in order to avoid the tax they would otherwise pay for the CO_2 they would otherwise emit. The use of similar techniques could be required for coal-fired generating plants, and can be used in combination with advanced approaches like integrated gasification combined cycle (IGCC). Even with the most advanced techniques, however, the economics of carbon capture and sequestration will depend upon the availability of and proximity to safe deep storage reservoirs. Nevertheless, it is time to recognize that the phrase "clean coal technology" is devoid of meaning unless it means "zero carbon emissions" technology.

CCS is only one of many new technological approaches that require a significant increase by governments and business in advanced research and development to speed the availability of more effective technologies that can help us solve the climate crisis more quickly. But it is important to emphasize that even without brand new technologies, we already have everything we need to get started on a solution to this crisis.

In a market economy like ours, however, every one of the solutions that I have discussed will be more effective and much easier to implement if we place a price on the CO_2 pollution that is recognized in the marketplace. We need to summon the courage to use the right tools for this job.

For the last fourteen years, I have advocated the elimination of all payroll taxes—including those for social security and unemployment compensation—and the replacement of that revenue in the form of pollution taxes—principally on CO_2. The overall level of taxation would remain exactly the same. It would be, in other words, a revenue neutral tax swap. But, instead of discouraging businesses from hiring more employees, it would discourage business from producing more pollution.

Global warming pollution, indeed all pollution, is now described by economists as an "externality." This absurd label means, in essence: we don't to keep track of this stuff so let's pretend it doesn't exist.

And sure enough, when it's not recognized in the marketplace, it does make it much easier for government, business, and all the rest of us to pretend that it doesn't exist. But what we're pretending doesn't exist is the stuff that is destroying the habitability of the planet. We put 70 million tons of it into the atmosphere every 24 hours and the amount is increasing day by day. Penalizing pollution instead of penalizing employment will work to reduce that pollution.

When we place a more accurate value on the consequences of the choices we make, our choices get better. At present, when business has to pay more taxes in order to hire more people, it is discouraged from hiring more people. If we change that and discourage them from creating more pollution they will reduce their pollution. Our market economy can help us solve this problem if we send it the right signals and tell ourselves the truth about the economic impact of pollution.

Many of our leading businesses are already making dramatic changes to reduce their global warming pollution. General Electric, Dupont, Cinergy, Caterpillar, and Wal-Mart are among the many who are providing leadership for the business community in helping us devise a solution for this crisis.

Leaders among unions—particularly the steel workers—have also added momentum to this growing movement.

Hunters and fishermen are also now adding their voices to the call for a solution to the crisis. In a recent poll, 86% of licensed hunters and anglers said that we have a moral obligation to stop global warming to protect our children's future.

And, young people—as they did during the Civil Rights Revolution—are confronting their elders with insistent questions about the morality of not moving swiftly to make these needed changes.

Moreover, the American religious community—including a group of 85 conservative evangelicals and especially the US Conference of Catholic Bishops—has made an extraordinary contribution to this entire enterprise. To the insights of science and technology, it has added the perspectives of faith and values, of prophetic imagination, spiritual motivation, and moral passion without which all our plans, no matter how reasonable, *simply will not prevail*. Individual faith groups have offered their own distinctive views. And yet—uniquely in religious life at this moment and even historically—they have established common ground and resolve across tenacious differences. In addition to reaching millions of people in the pews, they have demonstrated the real possibility of what we all now need to accomplish: how *to be ourselves, together* and how to discover, in this process, a sense of vivid, living spirit and purpose that elevates the entire human enterprise.

Individual Americans of all ages are becoming a part of a movement, asking what they can do as individuals and what they can do as consumers and as citizens and voters. Many individuals and businesses have decided to take an approach known as "Zero Carbon." They are reducing their CO_2 as much as possible and then offsetting the rest with reductions elsewhere including by the planting of trees. At least one entire community—Ballard, a city of 18,000 people in Washington State—is embarking on a goal of making the entire community zero carbon.

> This is not a political issue. This is a moral issue. It affects the survival of human civilization.

This is not a political issue. This is a moral issue. It affects the survival of human civilization. It is not a question of left vs. right; it is a question of right vs. wrong. Put simply, it is wrong to destroy the habitability of our planet and ruin the prospects of every generation that follows ours.

What is motivating millions of Americans to think differently about solutions to the climate crisis is the growing realization that this challenge is bringing us unprecedented opportunity. I have spoken before about the way the Chinese express the concept of crisis. They use two symbols, the first of which—by itself—means danger. The second, in isolation, means opportunity. Put them together, and you get "crisis." Our single word conveys the danger but doesn't always communicate the presence of opportunity in every crisis. In this case, the opportunity presented by the climate crisis is not only the opportunity for new and better jobs, new technologies, new opportunities for profit, and a higher quality of life. It gives us an opportunity to experience something that few generations ever have the privilege of knowing: a common moral purpose compelling enough to lift us above our limitations and motivate us to set aside some of the bickering to which we as human beings are naturally vulnerable. America's so-called "greatest generation" found such a purpose when they confronted the crisis of global fascism and won a war in Europe and in the Pacific simultaneously. In the process of achieving their historic victory, they found that they had gained new moral authority and a new capacity for vision. They created the

Marshall Plan and lifted their recently defeated adversaries from their knees and assisted them to a future of dignity and self-determination. They created the United Nations and the other global institutions that made possible many decades of prosperity, progress and relative peace. In recent years we have squandered that moral authority and it is high time to renew it by taking on the highest challenge of our generation. In rising to meet this challenge, we too will find self-renewal and transcendence and a new capacity for vision to see other crises in our time that cry out for solutions: 20 million HIV/AIDs orphans in Africa alone, civil wars fought by children, genocides and famines, the rape and pillage of our oceans and forests, an extinction crisis that threatens the web of life, and tens of millions of our fellow humans dying every year from easily preventable diseases. And, by rising to meet the climate crisis, we will find the vision and moral authority to see them not as political problems but as moral imperatives.

This is an opportunity for bipartisanship and transcendence, an opportunity to find our better selves and in rising to meet this challenge, create a better brighter future—a future worthy of the generations who come after us and who have a right to be able to depend on us.

Hot & Cold Media Spin Cycle

A Challenge to Journalists Who Cover Global Warming

James Inhofe

U.S. senator (R), Oklahoma 1995– ; born Des Moines, IA, November 17, 1934; B.A., University of Tulsa, 1973; served in the U.S. Army 1954–56; small businessman working in the fields of aviation, insurance, and real estate; elected to the Oklahoma State House of Representatives, 1966; served in the Oklahoma State Senate, 1969–1977; was selected as the Republican nominee for governor, 1974; ran for the U.S. House of Representatives, 1976; mayor of Tulsa, OK, 1978–84; U.S. representative (R), Oklahoma's First District, 1987–1995; elected to the U.S. Senate, 1994; U.S. Senate committees: Environment & Public Works (ranking member); Armed Services.

Editor's introduction: Senator Jim Inhofe, the ranking Republican on the U.S. Senate Committee on Environment & Public Works, is not only one of the foremost conservative voices in Congress, but also one of the most avid detractors of theories about global climate change. In this speech, delivered on the Senate Floor, he criticized the media for promoting the views of former Vice President Al Gore and other "alarmists," who "have pounded this mantra of 'consensus' on global warming into our pop culture." Inhofe points out that over the past century the media have trumpeted warnings about alternately forthcoming warming trends or ice ages—none of which have come to pass. As such, Inhofe argues, signing on to the Kyoto Protocol (an international treaty on climate change that requires the reduction of the emission of greenhouse gases) would not be worth the "economic pain"—particularly for the countries in Africa, Asia, and South America where many residents suffer from poverty and lack basic infrastructure.

James Inhofe's speech: I am going to speak today about the most media-hyped environmental issue of all time, global warming. I have spoken more about global warming than any other politician in Washington today. My speech will be a bit different from the previous seven floor speeches, as I focus not only on the science, but on the media's coverage of climate change.

Global Warming—just that term evokes many members in this chamber, the media, Hollywood elites and our pop culture to nod their heads and fret about an impending climate disaster. As the senator who has spent more time educating about the actual facts

---

Delivered on October 25, 2006, at Washington, D.C.

about global warming, I want to address some of the recent media coverage of global warming and Hollywood's involvement in the issue. And of course I will also discuss former Vice President Al Gore's movie "An Inconvenient Truth."

Since 1895, the media has alternated between global cooling and warming scares during four separate and sometimes overlapping time periods. From 1895 until the 1930's the media peddled a coming ice age.

From the late 1920's until the 1960's they warned of global warming. From the 1950's until the 1970's they warned us again of a coming ice age. This makes modern global warming the fourth estate's fourth attempt to promote opposing climate change fears during the last 100 years.

Recently, advocates of alarmism have grown increasingly desperate to try to convince the public that global warming is the greatest moral issue of our generation. Just last week, the vice president of London's Royal Society sent a chilling letter to the media encouraging them to stifle the voices of scientists skeptical of climate alarmism. During the past year, the American people have been served up an unprecedented parade of environmental alarmism by the media and entertainment industry, which link every possible weather event to global warming. The year 2006 saw many major organs of the media dismiss any pretense of balance and objectivity on climate change coverage and instead crossed squarely into global warming advocacy.

Summary of Latest Developments of Manmade Global Warming Hockey Stick

First, I would like to summarize some of the recent developments in the controversy over whether or not humans have created a climate catastrophe. One of the key aspects that the United Nations, environmental groups and the media have promoted as the "smoking gun" of proof of catastrophic global warming is the so-called 'hockey stick' temperature graph by climate scientist Michael Mann and his colleagues.

This graph purported to show that temperatures in the Northern Hemisphere remained relatively stable over 900 years, then spiked upward in the 20th century presumably due to human activity. Mann, who also co-publishes a global warming propaganda blog reportedly set up with the help of an environmental group, had his "Hockey Stick" come under severe scrutiny.

The "hockey stick" was completely and thoroughly broken once and for all in 2006. Several years ago, two Canadian researchers tore apart the statistical foundation for the hockey stick. In 2006, both the National Academy of Sciences and an independent researcher further refuted the foundation of the "hockey stick."

The National Academy of Sciences report reaffirmed the existence of the Medieval Warm Period from about 900 AD to 1300 AD and the Little Ice Age from about 1500 to 1850. Both of these periods occurred long before the invention of the SUV or human industrial activity could have possibly impacted the Earth's climate. In fact, scientists believe the Earth was warmer than today during the Medieval Warm Period, when the Vikings grew crops in Greenland.

Climate alarmists have been attempting to erase the inconvenient Medieval Warm Period from the Earth's climate history for at least a decade. David Deming, an assistant professor at the University of Oklahoma's College of Geosciences, can testify first hand about this effort.

Dr. Deming was welcomed into the close-knit group of global warming believers after he published a paper in 1995 that noted some warming in the 20th century. Deming says he was subsequently contacted by a prominent global warming alarmist and told point blank "We have to get rid of the Medieval Warm Period." When the "Hockey Stick" first appeared in 1998, it did just that.

End of Little Ice Age Means Warming

The media have missed the big pieces of the puzzle when it comes to the Earth's temperatures and mankind's carbon dioxide (CO_2) emissions. It is very simplistic to feign horror and say the one degree Fahrenheit temperature increase during the 20th century means we are all doomed. First of all, the one degree Fahrenheit rise coincided with the greatest advancement of living standards, life expectancy, food production and human health in the history of our planet. So it is hard to argue that the global warming we experienced in the 20th century was somehow negative or part of a catastrophic trend.

Second, what the climate alarmists and their advocates in the media have continued to ignore is the fact that the Little Ice Age, which resulted in harsh winters which froze New York Harbor and caused untold deaths, ended about 1850. So trying to prove man-made global warming by comparing the well-known fact that today's temperatures are warmer than during the Little Ice Age is akin to comparing summer to winter to show a catastrophic temperature trend.

In addition, something that the media almost never addresses are the holes in the theory that CO_2 has been the driving force in global warming. Alarmists fail to adequately explain why temperatures began warming at the end of the Little Ice Age in about 1850, long before man-made CO_2 emissions could have impacted the climate. Then about 1940, just as man-made CO_2 emissions rose sharply, the temperatures began a decline that lasted until the 1970's, prompting the media and many scientists to fear a coming ice age. Let me repeat, temperatures got colder after CO_2 emissions exploded. If CO_2 is the driving force of global climate change, why do so many in the media ignore the many skeptical scientists who cite these rather obvious inconvenient truths?

Sixty Scientists

My skeptical views on man-made catastrophic global warming have only strengthened as new science comes in. There have been recent findings in peer-reviewed literature over the last few years showing that the Antarctic is getting colder and the ice is growing and a new study in Geophysical Research Letters found that the sun was responsible for 50% of 20th century warming.

Recently, many scientists, including a leading member of the Russian Academy of Sciences, predicted long-term global cooling may be on the horizon due to a projected decrease in the sun's output.

A letter sent to the Canadian Prime Minister on April 6 of this year by 60 prominent scientists who question the basis for climate alarmism, clearly explains the current state of scientific knowledge on global warming.

The 60 scientists wrote:

"If, back in the mid-1990s, we knew what we know today about climate, Kyoto would almost certainly not exist, because we would have concluded it was not necessary." The letter also noted:

> "'Climate change is real' is a meaningless phrase used repeatedly by activists to convince the public that a climate catastrophe is looming and humanity is the cause. Neither of these fears is justified. Global climate changes occur all the time due to natural causes and the human impact still remains impossible to distinguish from this natural 'noise.'"

Computer Models Threaten Earth

One of the ways alarmists have pounded this mantra of "consensus" on global warming into our pop culture is through the use of computer models which project future calamity. But the science is simply not there to place so much faith in scary computer model scenarios which extrapolate the current and projected buildup of greenhouse gases in the atmosphere and conclude that the planet faces certain doom.

Dr. Vincent Gray, a research scientist and a 2001 reviewer with the UN's Intergovernmental Panel on Climate Change (IPCC) has noted, "The effects of aerosols, and their uncertainties, are such as to nullify completely the reliability of any of the climate models."

Earlier this year, the director of the International Arctic Research Center in Fairbanks Alaska, testified to Congress that highly publicized climate models showing a disappearing Arctic were nothing more than "science fiction."

In fact, after years of hearing about the computer generated scary scenarios about the future of our planet, I now believe that the greatest climate threat we face may be coming from alarmist computer models.

This threat is originating from the software installed on the hard drives of the publicity seeking climate modelers.

It is long past the time for us to separate climate change fact from hysteria.

Kyoto: Economic Pain for No Climate Gain

One final point on the science of climate change: I am approached by many in the media and others who ask, "What if you are wrong to doubt the dire global warming predictions? Will you be able to live with yourself for opposing the Kyoto Protocol?"

My answer is blunt. The history of the modern environmental movement is chock full of predictions of doom that never came true. We have all heard the dire predictions about the threat of overpopulation, resource scarcity, mass starvation, and the projected death of our oceans. None of these predictions came true, yet it never stopped the doomsayers from continuing to predict a dire environmental future.

The more the eco-doomsayers' predictions fail, the more the eco-doomsayers predict. These failed predictions are just one reason I respect the serious scientists out there today debunking the latest scaremongering on climate change. Scientists like MIT's Richard Lindzen, former Colorado State climatologist Roger Pielke, Sr., the University of Alabama's Roy Spencer and John Christy, Virginia State Climatologist Patrick Michaels, Colorado State University's William Gray, atmospheric physicist S. Fred Singer, Willie Soon of the Harvard-Smithsonian Center for Astrophysics, Oregon State climatologist George Taylor and astrophysicist Sallie Baliunas, to name a few.

But more importantly, it is the global warming alarmists who should be asked the question—"What if they are correct about man-made catastrophic global warming?"—because they have come up with no meaningful solution to their supposed climate crisis in the two decades that they have been hyping this issue.

If the alarmists truly believe that man-made greenhouse gas emissions are dooming the planet, then they must face up to the fact that symbolism does not solve a supposed climate crisis.

The alarmists freely concede that the Kyoto Protocol, even if fully ratified and complied with, would not have any meaningful impact on global temperatures. And keep in mind that Kyoto is not even close to being complied with by many of the nations that ratified it, including 13 of the EU-15 nations that are not going to meet their emission reduction promises.

Many of the nations that ratified Kyoto are now realizing what I have been saying all along: The Kyoto Protocol is a lot of economic pain for no climate gain.

Legislation that has been proposed in this chamber would have even less of a temperature effect than Kyoto's undetectable impact. And more recently, global warming alarmists and the media have been praising California for taking action to limit CO_2. But here again: This costly feel-good California measure, which is actually far less severe than Kyoto, will have no impact on the climate—only the economy.

Symbolism does not solve a climate crisis.

In addition, we now have many environmentalists and Hollywood celebrities, like Laurie David, who have been advocating measures like changing standard light bulbs in your home to fluorescents to help avert global warming. Changing to more energy-efficient light bulbs is a fine thing to do, but to somehow imply we can avert a climate disaster by these actions is absurd.

Once again, symbolism does not solve a climate crisis.

But this symbolism may be hiding a dark side. While greenhouse gas limiting proposals may cost the industrialized West trillions of dollars, it is the effect on the developing world's poor that is being lost in this debate.

The Kyoto Protocol's post 2012 agenda which mandates that the developing world be subjected to restrictions on greenhouse gases could have the potential to severely restrict development in regions of the world like Africa, Asia and South America—where some of the Earth's most energy-deprived people currently reside.

Expanding basic necessities like running water and electricity in the developing world are seen by many in the green movement as a threat to the planet's health that must be avoided.

Energy poverty equals a life of back-breaking poverty and premature death.

If we allow scientifically unfounded fears of global warming to influence policy makers to restrict future energy production and the creation of basic infrastructure in the developing world—billions of people will continue to suffer. Last week my committee heard testimony from Danish statistician Bjorn Lomborg, who was once a committed left-wing environmentalist until he realized that so much of what that movement preached was based on bad science. Lomborg wrote a book called "The Skeptical Environmentalist" and has organized some of the world's top Nobel Laureates to form the 2004 "Copenhagen Consensus" which ranked the world's most pressing problems. And guess what?

They placed global warming at the bottom of the list in terms of our planet's priorities. The "Copenhagen Consensus" found that the most important priorities of our planet included: combating disease, stopping malaria, securing clean water, and building infrastructure to help lift the developing nations out of poverty. I have made many trips to Africa, and once you see the devastating poverty that has a grip on that continent, you quickly realize that fears about global warming are severely misguided.

I firmly believe that when the history of our era is written, future generations will look back with puzzlement and wonder why we spent so much time and effort on global warming fears and pointless solutions like the Kyoto Protocol.

French President Jacques Chirac provided the key clue as to why so many in the international community still revere the Kyoto Protocol, who in 2000 said Kyoto represents "the first component of an authentic global governance."

Furthermore, if your goal is to limit CO_2 emissions, the only effective way to go about it is the use of cleaner, more efficient technologies that will meet the energy demands of this century and beyond.

The Bush administration and my Environment and Public Works Committee have been engaged in these efforts as we work to expand nuclear power and promote the Asia-Pacific Partnership. This partnership stresses the sharing of new technology among member nations including three of the world's top 10 emitters—China, India and North Korea—all of whom are exempt from Kyoto.

Media Coverage of Climate Change:

Many in the media, as I noted earlier, have taken it upon themselves to drop all pretense of balance on global warming and instead become committed advocates for the issue.

Here is a quote from *Newsweek* magazine:

"There are ominous signs that the Earth's weather patterns have begun to change dramatically and that these changes may portend a drastic decline in food production—with serious political implications for just about every nation on Earth."

A headline in the *New York Times* reads: "Climate Changes Endanger World's Food Output." Here is a quote from *Time Magazine*:

> "As they review the bizarre and unpredictable weather pattern of the past several years, a growing number of scientists are beginning to suspect that many seemingly contradictory meteorological fluctuations are actually part of a global climatic upheaval."

All of this sounds very ominous. That is, until you realize that the three quotes I just read were from articles in 1975 editions of *Newsweek Magazine* and *The New York Times*, and *Time Magazine* in 1974.

They weren't referring to global warming; they were warning of a coming ice age.

Let me repeat, all three of those quotes were published in the 1970's and warned of a coming ice age.

In addition to global cooling fears, *Time Magazine* has also reported on global warming. Here is an example:

> "[Those] who claim that winters were harder when they were boys are quite right . . . weathermen have no doubt that the world at least for the time being is growing warmer."

Before you think that this is just another example of the media promoting Vice President Gore's movie, you need to know that the quote I just read you from *Time Magazine* was not a recent quote; it was from January 2, 1939.

Yes, in 1939. Nine years before Vice President Gore was born and over three decades before *Time Magazine* began hyping a coming ice age and almost five decades before they returned to hyping global warming.

Time Magazine in 1951 pointed to receding permafrost in Russia as proof that the planet was warming.

In 1952, the *New York Times* noted that the "trump card" of global warming "has been the melting glaciers."

But Media Could Not Decide Between Warming or Cooling Scares

There are many more examples of the media and scientists flip-flopping between warming and cooling scares.

Here is a quote from the *New York Times* reporting on fears of an approaching ice age.

"Geologists Think the World May be Frozen Up Again."

That sentence appeared over 100 years ago in the February 24, 1895 edition of the *New York Times*.

Let me repeat. 1895, not 1995.

A front page article in the October 7, 1912 *New York Times*, just a few months after the Titanic struck an iceberg and sank, declared that a prominent professor "Warns Us of an Encroaching Ice Age."

The very same day in 1912, the *Los Angeles Times* ran an article warning that the "Human race will have to fight for its existence against cold."

An August 10, 1923 Washington Post article declared: "Ice Age Coming Here."

By the 1930's, the media took a break from reporting on the coming ice age and instead switched gears to promoting global warming:

"America in Longest Warm Spell Since 1776; Temperature Line Records a 25-year Rise" stated an article in the *New York Times* on March 27, 1933.

The media of yesteryear was also not above injecting large amounts of fear and alarmism into their climate articles.

An August 9, 1923 front page article in the *Chicago Tribune* declared:

"Scientist Says Arctic Ice Will Wipe Out Canada."

The article quoted a Yale University professor who predicted that large parts of Europe and Asia would be "wiped out" and Switzerland would be "entirely obliterated."

A December 29, 1974 *New York Times* article on global cooling reported that climatologists believed "the facts of the present climate change are such that the most optimistic experts would assign near certainty to major crop failure in a decade."

The article also warned that unless government officials reacted to the coming catastrophe, "mass deaths by starvation and probably in anarchy and violence" would result. In 1975, the *New York Times* reported that "A major cooling [was] widely considered to be inevitable."

These past predictions of doom have a familiar ring, don't they? They sound strikingly similar to our modern media promotion of the former vice president's brand of climate alarmism.

After more than a century of alternating between global cooling and warming, one would think that this media history would serve a cautionary tale for today's voices in the media and scientific community who are promoting yet another round of eco-doom.

Much of the 100-year media history on climate change that I have documented here today can be found in a publication titled "Fire and Ice" from the Business and Media Institute.

Media Coverage in 2006

Which raises the question: Has this embarrassing 100-year documented legacy of coverage on what turned out to be trendy climate science theories made the media more skeptical of today's sensational promoters of global warming? You be the judge.

On February 19th of this year, CBS News's "60 Minutes" produced a segment on the North Pole. The segment was a completely one-sided report, alleging rapid and unprecedented melting at the polar cap.

It even featured correspondent Scott Pelley claiming that the ice in Greenland was melting so fast, that he barely got off an ice-berg before it collapsed into the water.

"60 Minutes" failed to inform its viewers that a 2005 study by a scientist named Ola Johannessen and his colleagues showing that the interior of Greenland is gaining ice and mass and that according to scientists, the Arctic was warmer in the 1930's than today.

On March 19th of this year "60 Minutes" profiled NASA scientist and alarmist James Hansen, who was once again making allegations of being censored by the Bush administration. In this segment, objectivity and balance were again tossed aside in favor of a one-sided glowing profile of Hansen.

The "60 Minutes" segment made no mention of Hansen's partisan ties to former Democratic Vice President Al Gore or Hansen's receiving of a grant of a quarter of a million dollars from the left-wing Heinz Foundation run by Teresa Heinz Kerry. There was also no mention of Hansen's subsequent endorsement of her husband John Kerry for President in 2004.

Many in the media dwell on any industry support given to so-called climate skeptics, but the same media completely fail to note Hansen's huge grant from the left-wing Heinz Foundation.

The foundation's money originated from the Heinz family ketchup fortune. So it appears that the media makes a distinction between oil money and ketchup money.

"60 Minutes" also did not inform viewers that Hansen appeared to concede in a 2003 issue of Natural Science that the use of "extreme scenarios" to dramatize climate change "may have been appropriate at one time" to drive the public's attention to the issue.

Why would "60 Minutes" ignore the basic tenets of journalism, which call for objectivity and balance in sourcing, and do such one-sided segments?

The answer was provided by correspondent Scott Pelley. Pelley told the CBS News website that he justified excluding scientists skeptical of global warming alarmism from his segments because he considers skeptics to be the equivalent of "Holocaust deniers."

This year also saw a *New York Times* reporter write a children's book entitled "The North Pole Was Here." The author of the book, *New York Times* reporter Andrew Revkin, wrote that it may some-day be "easier to sail to than stand on" the North Pole in summer. So here we have a very prominent environmental reporter for the New York Times who is promoting aspects of global warming alarm-ism in a book aimed at children.

Time Magazine Hypes Alarmism

In April of this year, *Time Magazine* devoted an issue to global warming alarmism titled "Be Worried, Be Very Worried."

This is the same *Time Magazine* which first warned of a coming ice age in 1920's before switching to warning about global warming in the 1930's before switching yet again to promoting the 1970's coming ice age scare.

The April 3, 2006 global warming special report of *Time Magazine* was a prime example of the media's shortcomings, as the magazine cited partisan left-wing environmental groups with a vested finan-cial interest in hyping alarmism.

Headlines blared:

"More and More Land is Being Devastated by Drought"

"Earth at the Tipping Point"

"The Climate is Crashing,"

Time Magazine did not make the slightest attempt to balance its reporting with any views with scientists skeptical of this alleged cli-mate apocalypse.

I don't have journalism training, but I dare say calling a bunch of environmental groups with an obvious fund-raising agenda and ask-ing them to make wild speculations on how bad global warming might become, is nothing more than advocacy for their left-wing causes. It is a violation of basic journalistic standards.

To his credit, *New York Times* reporter Revkin saw fit to criticize *Time Magazine* for its embarrassing coverage of climate science.

So in the end, *Time*'s cover story title of "Be Worried, Be Very Wor-ried," appears to have been apt. The American people should be wor-ried—very worried—of such shoddy journalism.

Al Gore Inconvenient Truth

In May, our nation was exposed to perhaps one of the slickest science propaganda films of all time: former Vice President Gore's "An Inconvenient Truth." In addition to having the backing of Paramount Pictures to market this film, Gore had the full backing of the media, and leading the cheerleading charge was none other than the Associated Press.

On June 27, the Associated Press ran an article by Seth Borenstein that boldly declared "Scientists give two thumbs up to Gore's movie." The article quoted only five scientists praising Gore's science, despite AP's having contacted over 100 scientists.

The fact that over 80% of the scientists contacted by the AP had not even seen the movie or that many scientists have harshly criticized the science presented by Gore did not dissuade the news outlet one bit from its mission to promote Gore's brand of climate alarmism.

I am almost at a loss as to how to begin to address the series of errors, misleading science and unfounded speculation that appear in the former Vice President's film.

Here is what Richard Lindzen, a meteorologist from MIT has written about "An Inconvenient Truth."

> "A general characteristic of Mr. Gore's approach is to assiduously ignore the fact that the earth and its climate are dynamic; they are always changing even without any external forcing. To treat all change as something to fear is bad enough; to do so in order to exploit that fear is much worse."

What follows is a very brief summary of the science that the former Vice President promotes in either a wrong or misleading way:

- He promoted the now debunked "hockey stick" temperature chart in an attempt to prove man's overwhelming impact on the climate.

- He attempted to minimize the significance of Medieval Warm period and the Little Ice Age.

- He insisted on a link between increased hurricane activity and global warming that most scientists believe does not exist.

- He asserted that today's Arctic is experiencing unprecedented warmth while ignoring that temperatures in the 1930's were as warm or warmer.

- He claimed the Antarctic was warming and losing ice but failed to note, that is only true of a small region and the vast bulk has been cooling and gaining ice.

- He hyped unfounded fears that Greenland's ice is in danger of disappearing.

- He erroneously claimed that ice cap on Mt. Kilimanjaro is disappearing due to global warming, even while the region cools and researchers blame the ice loss on local land-use practices.

- He made assertions of massive future sea level rise that is way out side of any supposed scientific "consensus" and is not supported in even the most alarmist literature.

- He incorrectly implied that a Peruvian glacier's retreat is due to global warming, while ignoring the fact that the region has been cooling since the 1930s and other glaciers in South America are advancing.

- He blamed global warming for water loss in Africa's Lake Chad, despite NASA scientists concluding that local population and grazing factors are the more likely culprits.

- He inaccurately claimed polar bears are drowning in significant numbers due to melting ice when in fact they are thriving.

- He completely failed to inform viewers that the 48 scientists who accused President Bush of distorting science were part of a political advocacy group set up to support Democrat Presidential candidate John Kerry in 2004.

Now that was just a brief sampling of some of the errors presented in "An Inconvenient Truth." Imagine how long the list would have been if I had actually seen the movie—there would not be enough time to deliver this speech today.

Tom Brokaw

Following the promotion of "An Inconvenient Truth," the press did not miss a beat in their role as advocates for global warming fears.

ABC News put forth its best effort to secure its standing as an advocate for climate alarmism when the network put out a call for people to submit their anecdotal global warming horror stories in June for use in a future news segment.

In July, the Discovery Channel presented a documentary on global warming narrated by former NBC anchor Tom Brokaw. The program presented only those views of scientists promoting the idea that humans are destroying the Earth's climate.

You don't have to take my word for the program's overwhelming bias; a Bloomberg News TV review noted "You'll find more dissent at a North Korean political rally than in this program" because of its lack of scientific objectivity.

Brokaw also presented climate alarmist James Hansen to viewers as unbiased, failing to note his quarter million dollar grant form the partisan Heinz Foundation or his endorsement of Democrat Presidential nominee John Kerry in 2004 and his role promoting former Vice President Gore's Hollywood movie.

Brokaw, however, did find time to impugn the motives of scientists skeptical of climate alarmism when he featured paid environmental partisan Michael Oppenhimer of the group Environmental Defense accusing skeptics of being bought out by the fossil fuel interests.

The fact remains that political campaign funding by environmental groups to promote climate and environmental alarmism dwarfs spending by the fossil fuel industry by a three-to-one ratio. Environmental special interests, through their 527s, spent over $19 million compared to the $7 million that Oil and Gas spent through PACs in the 2004 election cycle.

I am reminded of a question the media often asks me about how much I have received in campaign contributions from the fossil fuel industry. My unapologetic answer is "Not Enough"—especially when you consider the millions partisan environmental groups pour into political campaigns.

Engineered "Consensus"

Continuing with our media analysis: On July 24, 2006 The *Los Angeles Times* featured an op-ed by Naomi Oreskes, a social scientist at the University of California San Diego and the author of a 2004 *Science Magazine* study. Oreskes insisted that a review of 928 scientific papers showed there was 100% consensus that global warming was not caused by natural climate variations. This study was also featured in former Vice President Gore's "An Inconvenient Truth."

However, the analysis in *Science Magazine* excluded nearly 11,000 studies or more than 90 percent of the papers dealing with global warming, according to a critique by British social scientist Benny Peiser.

Peiser also pointed out that less than two percent of the climate studies in the survey actually endorsed the so-called "consensus view" that human activity is driving global warming and some of the studies actually opposed that view.

But despite this manufactured "consensus," the media continued to ignore any attempt to question the orthodoxy of climate alarmism.

As the dog days of August rolled in, the American people were once again hit with more hot hype regarding global warming, this time from *The New York Times* op-ed pages. A columnist penned an August 3rd column filled with so many inaccuracies it is a wonder the editor of the Times saw fit to publish it.

For instance, Bob Herbert's column made dubious claims about polar bears, the snows of Kilimanjaro and he attempted to link this past summer's heat wave in the U.S. to global warming—something even alarmist James Hansen does not support.

Polar Bears Look Tired?

Finally, a September 15, 2006 Reuters News article claimed that polar bears in the Arctic are threatened with extinction by global warming. The article by correspondent Alister Doyle, quoted a visitor to the Arctic who claims he saw two distressed polar bears. According to the Reuters article, the man noted that "one of [the polar bears] looked to be dead and the other one looked to be exhausted."

The article did not state the bears were actually dead or exhausted, rather that they "looked" that way.

Have we really arrived at the point where major news outlets in the U.S. are reduced to analyzing whether or not polar bears in the Arctic appear restful?

How does reporting like this get approved for publication by the editors at Reuters?

What happened to covering the hard science of this issue?

What was missing from this Reuters news article was the fact that according to biologists who study the animals, polar bears are doing quite well. Biologist Dr. Mitchell Taylor from the Arctic government of Nunavut, a territory of Canada, refuted these claims in May when he noted that:

> "Of the 13 populations of polar bears in Canada, 11 are stable or increasing in number. They are not going extinct, or even appear to be affected at present."

Sadly, it appears that reporting anecdotes and hearsay as fact has now replaced the basic tenets of journalism for many media outlets.

Alarmism Has Led to Skepticism

It is an inconvenient truth that so far, 2006 has been a year in which major segments of the media have given up on any quest for journalistic balance, fairness and objectivity when it comes to climate change. The global warming alarmists and their friends in the media have attempted to smear scientists who dare question the premise of man-made catastrophic global warming, and as a result some scientists have seen their reputations and research funding dry up.

The media has so relentlessly promoted global warming fears that a British group called the Institute for Public Policy Research—and this from a left leaning group—issued a report in 2006 accusing media outlets of engaging in what they termed "climate porn" in order to attract the public's attention.

Bob Carter, a Paleoclimate geologist from James Cook University in Australia has described how the media promotes climate fear:

"Each such alarmist article is larded with words such as 'if,' 'might,' 'could,' 'probably,' 'perhaps,' 'expected,' 'projected' or 'modeled'—and many involve such deep dreaming, or ignorance of scientific facts and principles, that they are akin to nonsense," professor Carter concluded in an op-ed in April of this year.

Another example of this relentless hype is the reporting on the seemingly endless number of global warming impact studies which do not even address whether global warming is going to happen. They merely project the impact of potential temperature increases.

The media endlessly hypes studies that purportedly show that global warming could increase mosquito populations, malaria, West Nile Virus, heat waves and hurricanes, threaten the oceans, damage coral reefs, boost poison ivy growth, damage vineyards, and global food crops, to name just a few of the global warming linked calamities.

Oddly, according to the media reports, warmer temperatures almost never seem to have any positive effects on plant or animal life or food production.

Fortunately, the media's addiction to so-called 'climate porn' has failed to seduce many Americans.

According to a July Pew Research Center Poll, the American public is split about evenly between those who say global warming is due to human activity versus those who believe it's from natural factors or not happening at all. This is down from 85 percent just a year ago.

> We have a right to expect accuracy and objectivity on climate change coverage.

In addition, an August *Los Angeles Times/Bloomberg* poll found that most Americans do not attribute the cause of recent severe weather events to global warming, and the portion of Americans who believe global warming is naturally occurring is on the rise.

Yes—it appears that alarmism has led to skepticism.

The American people know when their intelligence is being insulted. They know when they are being used and when they are being duped by the hysterical left. The American people deserve better—much better—from our fourth estate. We have a right to expect accuracy and objectivity on climate change coverage. We have a right to expect balance in sourcing and fair analysis from reporters who cover the issue.

Above all, the media must roll back this mantra that there is scientific "consensus" of impending climatic doom as an excuse to ignore recent science. After all, there was a so-called scientific "consensus" that there were nine planets in our solar system until Pluto was recently demoted.

Breaking the cycles of media hysteria will not be easy since hysteria sells—it's very profitable. But I want to challenge the news media to reverse course and report on the objective science of climate change, to stop ignoring legitimate voices of this scientific debate and to stop acting as a vehicle for unsubstantiated hype.

A Time to Act

Dianne Feinstein

U.S. senator (D), California, 1992– ; born San Francisco, CA, June 22, 1933; B.A., history, Stanford University, 1955; appointed California Women's Parole Board, 1960–66; San Francisco Committee on Crime, 1968; elected first woman president, San Francisco County Board of Supervisors, 1970–78; first woman mayor, San Francisco, 1978–88; first woman elected U.S. senator from California; U.S. Senate committees: first woman member of the Senate Judiciary Committee; Appropriations; Select Committee on Intelligence; Rules and Administration (chair); other organizations: vice chair, C-Change: Collaborating to Conquer Cancer; chair, Senate Cancer Coalition; lead sponsor, Breast Cancer Research Stamp; awards and recognition: City and State Magazine's "Most Effective Mayor," 1987; Living Legacy Award 1987, Women's International Center; Woodrow Wilson Award for Public Service, 2001; first recipient, American Cancer Society's National Distinguished Advocacy Award, 2004.

Editor's introduction: In an effort to curb the emission of greenhouse gases and reduce the nation's dependence on foreign oil, Senator Dianne Feinstein introduced the Ten-in-Ten Fuel Economy Act on June 20, 2006. If passed, the legislation will raise CAFE (corporate average fuel economy), increasing the minimum fuel economy for passenger cars from 25 to 35 miles per gallon over the next 10 years. Attempts to improve CAFE standards usually draw protests from the automotive industry—even from Toyota, which manufactures the successful hybrid electric Prius. Nonetheless, Feinstein argues in the speech below, delivered at the Los Angeles, CA, Town Hall, that if we don't act now "the damage will be catastrophic and irreversible."

Dianne Feinstein's speech: Let me thank you for the introduction. Let me thank all of you for being here. I am particularly pleased that so many members of the Board of Supervisors, of the City Council, of government in one capacity or another could be here. I'm delighted that Fran Pavley, who has done so much on this issue and connecting issues, is here as well, because a lot of people have their head in the sand and really are not prepared to admit that, in fact, what is going on is going on. Today I'm here to discuss global warming. It is the single greatest environmental threat facing this planet. So let me explain the gravity of the problem.

Bottom line: The fuel we use to power our homes, our cars, our businesses, is causing the Earth to warm much faster than anyone expected. The first seven months of this year and the last three decades were the warmest in the United States since national

Delivered on October 25, 2006, at Los Angeles, CA.

record keeping began in 1895. This has been the warmest decade and it just goes on and on. Earth's temperature has climbed to the highest point it has been in the past 12,000 years.

First: How hot? If we act now and further temperature increases are kept to 1 to 2 degrees Fahrenheit by the end of this century, the damages, though significant, will be manageable. But if we don't act and warming increases by 5 to 9 degrees by the end of the century, the damage will be catastrophic and irreversible. Each of us is confronted with a choice, a choice that will not only impact our future but the future of our children and our grandchildren. Do we continue with the "business as usual" attitude or do we make the changes necessary to prevent catastrophe?

Now for the question: Why? Quite simply, because we are addicted to fossil fuels and it is the burning of these fuels—coal, oil, gasoline, natural gas and the greenhouse gases they produce—that is the primary cause of global warming. Carbon dioxide, the No. 1 global warming gas, is produced by power plants, cars, manufacturing and it is used to power residential and commercial buildings. Here is the key: Carbon dioxide does not dissipate in the atmosphere. It stays there for at least five decades that are known, causing the Earth's temperature to rise. This means that the carbon dioxide produced in the '50s, '60s, '70s, '80s, and '90s is still in the atmosphere today and the carbon dioxide produced today will still be in the atmosphere in 2050 and beyond. There will be serious consequences unless we make some changes. The problem is, we can't stop it. We can retard it. And that's the key. Leading scientists say that to stabilize the planet's climate by the end of this century we need a 70 percent reduction in carbon dioxide levels below 1990 levels and we need it by 2050. So the goals should be to stabilize carbon dioxide at 450 parts per billion. This could contain further warming to 1 to 2 degrees Fahrenheit. The Earth has warmed 1 degree in the past century.

Let me share with you some of the effects. Oceans are rising. Coral reefs are dying. Species are disappearing and glaciers all around the world are melting. We just learned last week that Greenland has lost 20 percent more mass than it receives from new snowfall each year and it will shrink further as the planet warms. Extreme weather patterns have emerged. This is one of the products, the offshoots of global warming. More volatility, heat waves, droughts, hurricanes, floods and they are occurring with greater frequency and greater volatility and intensity. In 2003, heat waves alone caused 20,000 deaths in Europe, 1,500 deaths in India and the number of Category 4 and 5 hurricanes has doubled since the 1970s. Katrina alone is testament to that. Things will only get worse as Earth's temperature rises. The question is, how much will that rise be? If nothing is done, if it's "business as usual" and Earth warms 5 to 9 degrees, the face of the planet changes forever. Now I meet so many people who believe the planet is immutable, that it can't change, but you have to know the planet has changed.

At one point, millions of years ago, we had one land mass. Look at Earth today and it's very interesting to go back in time and really look at how the land masses have moved around the globe and what caused that movement. So if the Earth warms with us doing nothing, Greenland and western Antarctica ice sheets will melt completely. These two ice sheets hold 20 percent of the Earth's fresh water. Sea levels could well rise by 20 feet. Think about that. Think about the damage that would cause to coastal areas around the world. Additionally, hurricanes, tornadoes and other severe weather would become more volatile than ever. Malaria would spread. Here in California, more than half of the Sierra Nevada snowpack will disappear. Now, that's equal to the water supply for 16 million people in this Southern California area. The rise in sea levels will cause catastrophic flooding and the Los Angeles basin will be especially vulnerable. Catastrophic wildfires will more than double. We had a mild taste of that future in July. Here in Los Angeles, temperatures spiked to over 100 degrees and it was worse in other areas of this state. I recently spent some time with five climatologists from Scripps Institution of Oceanography and they said to me—and they've read this speech and they agree with it—they said that if we have erred, we have been too conservative in our climate change estimates and the great worry they have is the Earth might tip earlier than predicted and, you see, once it tips you can't go back because you can't get these gases out of the atmosphere. So if we move beyond the tipping point, catastrophe becomes a certainty. That's why we should act soon and decisively. So now the question, well, what should we do?

We in the United States, a developed country, are 4 percent of the world's population. We use 25 percent of the world's energy. So we are a big producer. The largest contributor to global warming is electricity generation. That's 33 percent. Followed by transportation, which is 28 percent. These two sectors combine to make up 61 percent of the problem here in the United States. The remaining contributors are industry; big industries, about 20 percent, agriculture, about 7 percent, commercial properties, about 6.5 percent and residential, the same amount, 6.5 percent. What comes out of your house also produces CO_2, also warms the atmosphere. Let me be clear. There is no silver bullet. There is no one thing or another that can be done. Every business, every home, every industry must do its share and yes, every individual as well. So what can we do?

Let me begin with electricity generation. This is the largest single piece of the global warming puzzle, again responsible for 33 percent of global warming gases in our country. The biggest culprit in this sector is pulverized coal. Now, coal is the major source of electricity in 40 states so if coal refuses to change, multiply 40 by two United States senators and you see how difficult it is to move anything through the Senate of the United States. Coal alone, just coal, is 27 percent of annual carbon dioxide emissions, or 2.1 billion tons a year. Globally, coal produces 9.3 billion tons of CO_2 each year. That's one-third globally of all greenhouse gas emissions. So it is critical we find a way to clean up coal.

Earlier this year, the Senate Energy Committee, of which I'm a member, held a symposium and they had a number of experts come before them. The consensus of the experts was that a mandatory cap and trade program is, in fact, the most effective way forward. So we are working to create such a program. I would begin with two bills, one for electricity and one for the rest of large industry. Here's how it would work. We would cap the amount of global warming gases, including carbon dioxide and nitrous oxide and that cap would be established on all major emitters. In all likelihood, the cap would remain at this level for several years to give the industry the opportunity to make the necessary changes. Gradually, over time, the caps would be tightened and emissions reduced. Now electricity producers would have two ways of meeting the cap. They could either implement new technologies or they could purchase what's called a credit, or an allowance, from other companies that have reduced their emissions below the target cap. Or they can do both. So the cap would be met and carbon dioxide would be ratcheted down over time. One of the key elements of the bill I intend to introduce is allowing agriculture to participate. Farmers, growers, foresters will be able to earn credits, or dollars, for moving to greener farming practices. These include changing their tilling practices. The Earth releases carbon dioxide—planting trees on vacant land, converting crops to those that can be used for biofuels, for example, cellulosic ethanol, switch grass, energy producing crops. Farmers and growers would be able to earn dollars from acres converted to carbon sequestration and reduction.

Next we need to include other major industrial producers of carbon dioxide in a similar regime. Now, many people say OK, a cap and trade, it's a new thing, I'm not quite sure. Well, cap and trade has been used before. Under the Clean Air Act, remember acid rain? A cap and trade regime was implemented in the 1980s to reduce sulfur dioxide and nitrogen oxide emissions from electric utility plants in the Northeast. These are the primary culprits of acid rain. In the 16 years since, this protocol has reduced sulfur dioxide emissions by 34 percent. That's 5 million tons—and nitrogen oxide emissions by 43 percent. That's 3 million tons. So cap and trade can work. The key is getting it in place and getting the technologies moving, creating the incentives to do it. Now the governors of seven Northeastern states are instituting their own cap and trade system. You may have read Governor Schwarzenegger went back to meet with Governor Pataki to talk about California participating in this, the Northeast regime's cap and trade system. It goes online in 2008. I have been negotiating this, my bill, with a group called the Clean Energy Group. Remember I mentioned how dominant coal is in 40 states and how difficult it is to get the votes? Well, I've come to the conclusion that I want to work with part of the electricity sector that is prepared to move and will sit down and negotiate and they have cap levels. The Clean Energy Group includes Pacific Gas and Electric, Florida Power and Light, Entergy, Calpine, and the Public Services Enterprise Group. These companies produce 15 percent of the energy nationwide, 150,000 megawatts or energy for 150 million homes. So I hope that they will come out in full force in support of this and we will then be able to pass this bill in the Senate, at least in the United States.

Let me take up transportation: cars, trucks, planes, cargo ships. They represent 28 percent of carbon dioxide emissions. Passenger vehicles alone—cars, light trucks and SUVs—make up 20 percent of all United States emissions. That's 1.2 million tons. Fundamentally, there are two ways to reduce these emissions. (1) Improve the fuel efficiency of these vehicles and (2) move away from oil- and gasoline-based fuels toward alternatives. I believe we need to do both. The good news is that the technology exists to significantly improve the fuel economy of these vehicles. You know, you read the troubles that Ford is having and they're going to take a good look at really a major change in their industry. I would really urge them, go green. The future is green and there are all kinds of ways to do it. The bad news is that Detroit and some foreign automakers refuse to utilize the technologies that exist today. Senator Olympia Snowe and I have introduced a bipartisan bill which would require the mileage of all cars, pickup trucks and SUVs to be increased from 25 to 35 miles per gallon over the next 10 years. We call it 10 over 10. If this bill becomes law, we would save 420 metric tons of carbon dioxide by 2025. Now let me relate that to something you might understand. That's the equivalent of the exact amount of oil we import from the Middle East today—2.5 million barrels of oil a day. So that in and of itself would be significant. The other side of the transportation coin is new technologies and alternative fuels and this is really an exciting part. As long as our nation continues our addiction to oil we cannot sufficiently slow the global warming trend. That's why we need to develop new clean technologies and alternative fuels. This includes the electric plug-in hybrid, biofuels, and ethanol 85 using cellulosic ethanol and fuel cells.

The good news is there is substantial venture capital funding to invest in clean energy projects. Last Monday I spoke to 200 Silicon Valley CEOs, all of whom then signed an energy pledge, all of whom want to participate in this burgeoning new area of endeavor. I also visited a Silicon Valley startup called Bloom Energy and they're developing fuel cells. Well, let me show you a fuel cell. This is a fuel cell. On one side is cathode ink and on the other side is anode ink. The substance in the middle is coated with a zirconium sand and this one fuel cell is enough to light a 30-watt bulb for five years.

> As long as our nation continues our addiction to oil we cannot sufficiently slow the global warming trend.

Now, if you put these fuel cells together in a fuel cell block encased about the size of something that would be this high and fit in a parking space, it will power a 20,000-square-foot building. So you'd be able to, in the future, power subdivisions with fuel cells, to power individual homes with small fuel cells. This is one of the creative inventions that are taking place. It's my understanding that Bill Gates has joined with venture capitalist Vinod Khosla to spearhead investment efforts in ethanol plants which when completed will produce 220 million gallons by 2009. Now I wanted to say one thing. Corn ethanol is not the answer. Corn ethanol has an inverse energy ratio, but cellulosic ethanol is the answer and can be produced. Others are investing in new ideas: inexpensive solar panels, windmills that can be built in your backyard for $10,000 and geothermal energy that harnesses the heat of the Earth. Chevron has formed a strategic search alliance with the National Renewable Energy Lab in Colorado to advance the development of biofuels. I say good for Chevron. We ought to encourage it. It's also working with scientists at UC Davis to develop cellulosic ethanol. I say great. And Los Angeles has become a climate action leader and has registered its greenhouse gases and will be seeking to reduce its emissions. These efforts are important and I really urge you to support them.

But America needs to be much more energy efficient as well, both in terms of green building codes and individual conservation and energy use. An aggressive national emergency efficiency program patterned after California's successful one could prevent a substantial amount of carbon dioxide from going into the air. This is the third prong of my proposal and it would come from the incorporation of energy efficient building materials in a construction such as insulation, more efficient windows, renewable technologies like solar and wind. An initial $100,000 investment in green construction can result in a $1 million or more savings over the life of a building that's 20,000 square feet—and the bigger the building the bigger the saving. So, green energy is cost effective. Individuals can make a difference. You can make a difference. I can make a difference. This means carpooling, using energy-efficient light bulbs. A 30-watt new fluorescent bulb produces equal to a 100-watt incandescent bulb. Use them in your home. Buy Energy Star refrigerators, dishwashers, phones, DVD players, televisions. These should become standard for every American.

In 2005 alone, these products, energy-saving products, saved consumers $12 billion and reduced emissions by nearly 5 percent. These are easy to do and they make a difference. So, early on in the next Congress, the 110th, which begins in January, I will be introducing the following legislation: a mandatory cap and trade program as I discussed with you for electricity and one for other industries, the 10-over-10 bill requiring the increased mileage of 10 miles per gallon in the next 10 years, an alternative fuels bill that requires 70 percent of all vehicles produced after a certain year to be flex-fuel capable—the cost is small, it's $100 a vehicle, it could be done right now to the existing fleet of automobiles. These vehicles also will be required to have a green gas cap to show the owner that the car can, in fact, accept other fuels. We would also require that gasoline stations owned and operated by major oil companies have at least one pump that provides alternative fuels at every station. The fourth bill will be a national energy efficiency program including appliance and building standards requiring utilities to use energy efficiency measures, to meet their portion of demand. And we will also strive to eliminate a very protectionist tariff that was put in the debate over corn ethanol and at the urging of the Midwest corn farmers, a 54 percent per gallon tariff on imported ethanol was put into law to prevent cheaper alternative ethanol from coming into the country. It is estimated, for example, that Brazilian E-85 ethanol will be much cheaper and will work much better. Senator Craig Thomas and I are working on a plan to use Wyoming Powder River coal in a pilot to see if carbon sequestration from coal plants can actually work. The pilot would be set up and if it works, there are lines to bring that power into the west, which would be part of the agreement. The *Los Angeles Times* this morning had a very interesting story about UC partnering to try to do a pilot in coal sequestration right here in California. The big lacking, I think, is when these pilots take place or when there is a coal gasification or sequestration plan, that it be monitored by an independent authority and I think we will probably need to have some legislation to be sure that's the case.

Now, we can't do this alone. It's a big planet out there and the whole planet is affected. The United States must make addressing global warming a top priority. We must join the European Union and other nations in reducing emissions. Here's why. United States today leads in the production of greenhouse gases but we're closely followed by China, Europe, Russia, Japan and India. So, all countries must participate. The Kyoto Protocol is not perfect; it will expire in 2012. The United States can't have its head in the sand. We are either a leader in this or we're not and no one's going to listen to us unless we begin and we don't say, you know, do as we say, we say do as we do. China is greatly concerning. China's coal use outpaces that of the United States, the EU and Japan combined. Coal accounts for 70 percent of China's energy needs, and she is building a new dirty, pulverized coal power plant every week, week in and week out. China is soon going to pass the United States as the biggest emitter of carbon dioxide. If it continues its course, it could cause carbon dioxide levels to quadruple so it is vital that we engage China in a public/private partnership that funds key carbon dioxide reduction projects on a bilateral basis.

I've spoken about this in other places and it's interesting, there's a great deal of interest. McKenzie & Co., we had a session in Aspen, the Aspen Strategy Institute, on a seminar on China rising and the director of McKenzie & Co. said we'd be interested in participating. Goldman Sachs, the director there, said we'd be interested in participating. There is a need, and I think maybe Silicon Valley provides the lead with venture capital to put together some joint ventures to really begin alternatives to dirty coal production in China. Bottom line in the end—now is the time to begin to act and that's why I'm talking to you and that's why I go all over wherever I can to talk to you. Let the members of the House and Senate know that you want action. Right now the mentality is do nothing. It won't work. The choice is clear. It's time to stop talking and begin acting. So, I'm here to say will you help? If you can support these bills we'll make them available to you. You can take a look at them, and if you like them, please weigh in. Thank you.

Remarks at the Natural Resources Committee Meeting of the National Governors Association (NGA)

Stephen L. Johnson

Administrator of the U.S. Environmental Protection Agency (EPA), 2005– ; born Washington, D.C., March 21, 1951; B.A., biology, Taylor University, 1972; M.S., pathology, George Washington University, 1976; director of operations, Litton Bionetics, 1976–80; senior science adviser, EPA, 1980–84, 1986–88; director of operations, Hazleton Laboratories Corporation, 1984–86; director, Field Operations Division, Office of Pesticide Programs (OPP), EPA, 1984–86; deputy director, Hazard Evaluation Division, OPP, EPA, 1988–90; chairman, Federal Insecticide, Fungicide, and Rodenticide Act science advisory panel, EPA, 1988–90; director, Registration Division, EPA, Washington, D.C.; deputy director, OPP, EPA, 1997–99; assistant administrator, Office of Prevention, Pesticides, and Toxic Substances (OPPTS), EPA, 2000–03; acting deputy administrator, EPA, 2003–04; deputy administrator, EPA, 2004–05; acting administrator, EPA, 2005.

Editor's introduction: As the head of the Environmental Protection Agency (EPA), Stephen L. Johnson is charged with protecting human health and the environment. He was the only Bush administration official in attendance at the National Governors Association's annual meeting in 2007, and as such "got an earful from governors frustrated over what they see as EPA's foot-dragging on several energy issues," according to Pamela M. Prah, reporting for *Stateline.org*. Critics have frequently lamented the Bush administration's environmental record, claiming that the president has turned a blind eye to global warming and other threats. Nonetheless, Johnson assured the governors that the president intends to address global climate changes and understands that "only a global strategy will sufficiently tackle this global challenge."

Steve Johnson's speech: Thank you, Governor Schweitzer, for that introduction. Because of the collaborative work of NGA and governors across this country, our nation's air, water and land are cleaner today than they were just a generation ago. I appreciate you inviting me to address an issue of concern to all of us—global climate change.

The challenge of global climate change is exactly that: global.

With developing countries like India and China soon catching and surpassing greenhouse gas emissions from developed countries, only a global strategy will sufficiently tackle this global challenge.

Delivered on July 22, 2007, at Traverse City, MI.

President Bush understands this as well. And during the recent meeting of the G8, he called upon the world's economic leaders to set a global goal on long-term greenhouse gas reductions. Members of the G8 reached an agreement on a process for rapidly developing and concluding a new comprehensive, post-Kyoto accord on climate change, energy-efficiency, and energy securitys. Under the framework, each country would establish midterm national targets and programs that reflect their own current and future energy needs. The framework also emphasizes the importance of transparency and accountability. The President believes that by encouraging and sharing cutting-edge technologies, major economic leaders can meet realistic reduction goals.

America is committed to being a good global neighbor. And over the past six years, the Bush Administration has been working with our international partners, helping them understand that environmental protection and economic progress can, and do, go hand in hand.

We at EPA are pleased to be a major player in this effort by investing in the international partnerships that are delivering real global results.

Take, for example, the Asia-Pacific Partnership on Clean Development and Climate. Through this international collaboration, EPA is working with six countries—Australia, China, India, Japan, Republic of Korea, and the U.S.—which collectively account for about half of the world's economic output, population, and energy use. Under the partnership, we are helping these countries and the private sector expand investment and trade in cleaner energy technologies, goods, and services in key market sectors.

Another program is the Methane to Markets Partnership. Launched in November 2004, this partnership of 20 countries and more than 500 public and private sector partners is working to reduce greenhouse gas emissions by capturing and utilizing methane as a cleaner source of energy. In doing so, Methane to Markets is promoting energy security, economic growth, cleaner air, and reductions in greenhouse-gas emissions around the world.

These international efforts are just one aspect of our nation's unparalleled commitments to the reduction of greenhouse gas emissions.

Global climate change is a challenge this Administration takes seriously. So much so, that since 2001, our nation has invested over $37 billion to advance climate change science, expand innovative technologies and establish tax-incentive programs. That's more than any other country in the world.

We're working on real and significant initiatives that will improve our energy efficiency, enhance our energy security and reduce domestic emissions of greenhouse gases. And we're doing it on three different fronts.

The first is the transportation sector, which accounts for approximately one-third of our national greenhouse gas emissions.

There's been a lot of news recently about this effort, specifically regarding the President's Twenty-in-Ten legislative plan.

Announced in the State of the Union Address, the President's plan would reduce U.S. gasoline consumption by 20 percent in the next ten years, and calls on the country to increase renewable and alternative fuel use to 35 billion gallons during that time. It would also reform the CAFE standards.

While the Administration is working with Congress to enact his plan, in May, the President directed us to move ahead and take the first regulatory step to address greenhouse gas emissions from cars. We're working across agencies to develop a proposed regulation under the Clean Air Act by the end of this year, with final rules due out by the end of next year. This is an aggressive pace for developing any rule, let alone rules of this magnitude.

I will also make a decision by the end of this calendar year on the California petition. With two public hearings, 34,000 comments and hundreds of pages of technical and scientific analysis, we are expeditiously, but responsibly, addressing the petition.

And while implementing the President's directive may be a first step toward addressing the Supreme Court's decision—it is far from our first step of reducing the greenhouse gas emissions that contribute to climate change.

Across the Administration, we are investing in a wide array of partnerships, which rely on voluntary measures to reduce greenhouse gas emissions and remove barriers to the introduction of cleaner technologies.

> It is important that we manage our nation's large reserves of coal in an environmentally responsible manner.

Some of these partnerships are helping cut the release of greenhouse gases from the power sector—responsible for approximately 40 percent of our domestic emissions.

Coal-fired power plants are an important player in this effort. Currently, about 50 percent of the electricity in the United States is generated from coal. And, at current rates of consumption, our nation's coal reserves are large enough to meet our energy needs for more than 200 years. To achieve the Administration's ambitious energy security goals, coal must continue to play a major role in the generation of electricity in this country. But it is important that we manage our nation's large reserves of coal in an environmentally responsible manner.

EPA, the Department of Energy and others are currently exploring ways to burn coal more efficiently and with fewer emissions. In addition, we are seeing technologies such as carbon capture and storage that have the potential to significantly reduce greenhouse gas emissions from coal-fired electricity generation, while allowing continued use of our ample coal reserves.

From pilot studies to evaluate carbon sequestration technologies, to building the first nearly zero emission coal fired power plant, called FutureGen, our nation is addressing its growing energy demand in a way that supports the goals for a clean environment and a healthy economy.

At EPA, we see environmental responsibility as everyone's responsibility . . . so we're helping Americans make smart decisions about how they purchase and use energy.

This brings me to the final piece of the greenhouse gas puzzle—individual consumers and the industry sector.

Today, nearly everyone has heard of Energy Star—the label that signals to consumers that a product is energy-efficient. This common-sense program encourages businesses and consumers to make energy-efficient choices that are good for the environment and good for the bottom line.

In 2006 alone, by purchasing Energy Star products, Americans saved $14 billion on their utility bills, and prevented greenhouse gas emissions equivalent to those from 25 million cars—that's more than all the cars in the states represented in NGA's Natural Resources Committee combined.

Our campaign Energy Star Change a Light, Change the World, is a national call-to-action to encourage every individual to help change the world, one light at a time. Going into its 8th year, the campaign kicks off on Wednesday, October 3rd. Our partners across the nation will help celebrate this day with activities, events, government proclamations, and in-store promotions around energy-efficient lighting.

To date, more than half a million Americans have pledged to replace over 1.1 million lights with Energy Star lights, preventing over 460 million pounds of greenhouse gas emissions and saving over 320 kilowatt hours and nearly $30 million in energy costs. This year—with your help—we can do even better. I challenge every state to declare October 3, Energy Star Change a Light Day, and help us brighten America's future literally one light at a time.

While we work to change the way Americans use their power, we're also helping them change the type of power they purchase.

Under EPA's Green Power Partnership, we're driving demand for green power nationwide by encouraging an ever-increasing number of organizations to buy green power. To date, more than 750 organizations are purchasing nearly 10 billion kilowatt-hours of green power annually. Not only is EPA the founder of this program, but we now purchase 100 percent green power for our facilities.

The Green Power program is growing rapidly. Currently, seven states partners are voluntarily buying more than 126 million kilowatt-hours of green power annually.

In addition, many state and local governments are enacting clean energy policies that save energy and improve air quality. To date, 16 states have implemented or proposed statewide greenhouse gas targets . . . 10 states have implemented an energy efficiency portfolio standard . . . and 24 states have implemented a renewable portfolio standard. And with your help, these numbers will continue to grow.

But as you know, greenhouse gases include more than carbon dioxide—and we have partnership programs to help our state, local and industry partners address those as well. The Administration's suite of methane programs—focusing on coal mines, landfills, and natural gas systems—have contributed to reducing emissions of methane by more than 10 percent below 1990 levels. This success led to the formation of the international Methane to Markets Partnership, which I mentioned earlier.

Operating in over half the states in the nation, our Landfill Methane Outreach Program has helped develop more than 325 landfill gas energy projects, reducing methane emissions by over 27 million metric tons of carbon equivalent. EPA estimates that at least 560 additional landfills nationwide present attractive opportunities for methane reductions. As Governors, you are in a unique position to help us utilize our nation's landfills as a potential source of clean energy.

Coal mines present another opportunity for methane capture. That's why EPA is supporting the first-ever U.S. demonstration of a technology to mitigate methane emissions from coal mine ventilation air, which will be conducted at an abandoned mine in West Virginia.

So what do all these programs with consumers and the transportation, energy and industry sectors really mean? Well, put simply, they are delivering real environmental results.

According to EPA data reported to the United Nations Framework Convention on Climate Change, U.S. greenhouse gas intensity declined by 1.9 percent in 2003 and by 2.4 percent in both 2004 and 2005. Looking at it another way, from 2004 to 2005, the U.S. economy grew by 3.2 percent, while greenhouse gas emissions increased by only 0.8 percent.

Both at home and abroad, we are implementing an aggressive yet practical strategy to reduce global greenhouse gas emissions, protect the American economy, and engage the developing world.

As we consider new technologies and new strategies, it is essential for us to learn from the lessons of programs we have implemented at the federal, state and local levels.

Global, national and local collaboration is essential as we work to develop a clean, secure energy future. It is my hope that each of us will do our part to encourage solutions that are good for our environment, good for our economy, and good for our energy security.

Thank you, and I would be happy to answer any questions the governors may have.

Cumulative Speaker Index: 2000–2007

A cumulative speaker index to the volumes of *Representative American Speeches* for the years 1937–1938 through 1959–1960 appears in the 1959–1960 volume; for the years 1960–1961 through 1969–1970, see the 1969–1970 volume; for the years 1970–1971 through 1979–1980, see the 1979–1980 volume; for the years 1980–1981 through 1989–1990, see the 1989–1990 volume; and for the years 1990–1991 through 1999–2000, see the 1999–2000 volume.

Index